24

SECRETS TO
GREAT PARENTING

Jim and Bonnie Inkster
Tried, Tested and True

A CIP catalogue record for this title is available from the British library.
ISBN 978-0-9563342-0-6

Design concept by Affi Luc Agbodo, Affi Luc Ltd
Cover design by Becky Doggett
Formatted by Affi Luc Agbodo and Becky Doggett
Photography by Emmanuel Ruhumuriza, Idrawwithlight
Printed and bound by MPG Biddles

5 Smooth Stones
136 Linden Road
Birmingham
B30 1LB

We dedicate this book to our four wonderful children:
Joel
Becky
Jared
Jessica
We love you so very much. You have brought great joy into our lives and the lives of many, many others. You are the best.

About the Authors:

Jim and Bonnie Inkster have been married for 38 years at the time of publication. They have had the joy of raising four children together over a 30-year period. Their family is their abiding passion, ever expanding to now include seven grandchildren.

Jim and Bonnie Inkster lived in Canada until 1999 when they moved with their two youngest children to England. They have been educators as well as community leaders. In 2000 they started a leadership training college in Essex. They love to teach and train people to reach their potential and to truly enjoy life.

They speak at seminars and conferences worldwide. They conduct seminars on marriage, parenting, leadership and a host of other topics.

Table of Contents

The First Word

Do you remember when you first decided to have children? You had probably been broody for a while. Come on guys even my sons have admitted to being broody! Everywhere you looked there were mothers with newborns in cute little outfits, hand knitted jumpers and sweet little bonnets. You made the fatal mistake of holding your friend's little ones. Did you know that babies are contagious? Particularly to women! That's right! I have watched it happen over and over again. A young woman holding a friend's baby will vehemently deny that there is any possibility that she and her partner are going to have children. Countless times I have witnessed this denial and then, the soon to follow announcement of pregnancy.

Usually we get to hold them when they are just fed, burped and contented or have fallen asleep. You are absolutely convinced that

1

heaven opened on the day of this child's birth and released an angel. What bliss, what joy, what ultimate delusion! It has to happen or the human race would probably cease to exist. Now here you are reading the introduction to a book on parenting. Obviously heaven had a hiccup and reality set in. You have found your lovely gift from above has a will all their own. Like every other member of the human race they want everything their way.

Don't worry! Parenting is not an innate gift that some have and others don't. Parenting is a learned skill and one that can be passed on from generation to generation. The only problem with that is bad parenting can be passed on as well as good. The good news is that parenting is learned so you can do something about the quality of skills that may have been passed on to you. Changing a bad skill for a good one requires that you recognise that what you are doing is not working and you are desperate enough to change.

Before you read any further you also have to understand that there is no such thing as a perfect parent. All parents make mistakes. But mistakes can be corrected and learned from. Even if you were perfect, you would still be found wanting in something you had done. You see your child does not see everything from your perspective. They won't have the information or necessarily the maturity to

2

make the correct decisions that are required in a situation. That's one of the reasons why they have parents. So at some time or another you may be seen as Attila the Hun in the eyes of your child. Get used to it. You are there for their good whether it's appreciated or not. If you develop a strong relationship with your child where communication is clear, there will be plenty of opportunities to talk over situations that may have seemed unjust to them in the moment. Relax in the knowledge that you will make mistakes but they are not irreversible.

A few years ago a friend who was greatly influenced by observing our family challenged us by asking what we were doing to share the ability that we had in the area of childrearing. He said that over the years we might influence a circle of 300 or maybe more friends and acquaintances. But that we had something much more valuable to be shared with many more people than that. So this book is our attempt to share some of our experience with others. We waited to write about parenting until our children were adults. What is the point of talking like an expert when you still have children who haven't passed through the teen years? We also didn't want to put our children under the kind of scrutiny they would have had to face if we had published something. It is tough enough growing up as it is! Our four children have survived that and have grown to be wonderful adults whose company we love. They experienced life fully and yet were great kids through their teen years.

Because of our own experience as parents and because of the situations we see with young parents, we felt compelled to write this book. In our creating the outline we were looking at some of the teaching material that we had used in seminars. This material gives succinct and fundamental actions that can be applied immediately to bring about effective changes in your children's lives. With that in mind and having started our life as parents with twins, we learned to appreciate most things that were short and to the point. We also developed a liking for burned toast and popcorn. Really, most everything charred now rates up there as ok with us.

Often the only place of refuge one could find was the bathroom or toilet where possibly you might get a few minutes to yourself. With that in mind we decided to write a survival guide for parents that they could read in the loo. Each chapter is intended to give you a new insight to add to your toolkit for childrearing so that you will truly enjoy the experience and be recognised by others, including your own children, as good parents.

Over the years we have seen how one

change can create a huge impact in the quality of one's life. Each chapter has life changing effects when given the appropriate time to be implemented. May we suggest you apply one idea effectively before going onto the next one? In 24 weeks you will have worked through the entire book and transformed your family life.

So without further ado let us begin.

Do You Want Change?

Are there things that your child is doing that are driving you crazy? Do you wish you had been more corrective of their behaviour earlier and now things are getting out of hand? One of the things we have encountered in teaching seminars on marriage or childrearing is that people want answers to specific behaviour problems NOW. One couple once told us that they knew all the things not to do to get into trouble in marriage. What they wanted to know was how to get out of trouble now that they were in it. Parents usually come to the course because they have problems that they want to fix now. So laying the groundwork for what to do is usually not what they want to hear. It's: "Help, I'm in trouble now, get me out of it."

Before I say anything else about creating change let me give you the answer. **CHANGE**

ONE THING AT A TIME.

We attended a church for a time where they would sing songs that had been sung every week for the last ten years. The song leader would get very frustrated and bring in 10 new songs on a Sunday. No one knew the songs so there wasn't a great deal of volume or enthusiasm in the singing. That would disappoint him so the next week he would revert to all the old songs. This cycle happened every two months for a year. He would introduce all the new songs one week, then go back to the old for seven weeks. From our perspective the problem was simple. By changing all the songs at once we were overwhelmed. He would get frustrated by our lack of response and go back to the way it was. If he had introduced one new song a week and repeated it again the next week, we could have learnt all the new material. But he kept following this futile method that eventually led to him resigning his position.

Many parents do that with their children. They decide they have had enough; it can't go on like this any longer. So they attack change with a vengeance and simply overwhelm their child. Their child can't cope and acts worse than before. The parents then throw up their hands in despair and throw in the towel in their effort to bring change. Just like the song leader they go back to the way it was. Inside they are still frustrated, in fact, probably more than before. Bonnie was asked once to talk to a mother of four who was having difficulty with her children's behaviour. Every time Bonnie suggested anything the mother would say, 'Oh, we tried that and it didn't work'. She probably had but had tried to change too many things at one time.

Children, even adults too, have trouble handling more than one thing at a time. Have you seen that chart for figuring out your stress levels? Major events add incredible levels of stress that can overload an individual and cause a breakdown or heart attack. Some stress is considered necessary to our daily functioning but too much creates problems. Remember when you started a new job and there were all those tasks that seemed so onerous at the time. You would be sweating and shaky when you had to serve your first customer. You would even make excuses or clarify that it was your first day so they would give you some space to handle the situation. Your child needs to be given room to change and adapt to the new demands.

When I was training to be a teacher, my supervisor watched me writing some instructions on the blackboard. He told me how good my writing was, made a suggestion for a slight change to my 'e' and then told me once again how good my writing was. I had no problem making the change. He then gloated about how well the technique that he called a 'praise sandwich' worked. You sandwich any change within two doses of praise for the things they are doing right.

If you want to change your child's behaviour, then you must focus on only one issue at a time. Make sure it is the most important one to you. Don't worry what others think. Choose the issue that causes you the most stress and work on that. You owe it to your child and yourself to change the one that causes you to be a bear. You'll find you're happier and your child will be happier. Once that one is corrected you can choose another. That way you see progress and you won't give up. Remember: **CHANGE ONLY ONE THING AT A TIME!**

POINTS TO PONDER

1. *Is there an area in your child's life that you want to see changed?*

2. *Try to identify the cause and source of the behaviour you would like changed.*

3. *Talk to someone else about the behaviour and possible source to see if you have a proper perspective on the issue.*

4. *What can you do to encourage a change in behaviour?*

You Want To Do What!

Good children don't just happen, they take work. Part of that work is to know what matters to you. What is important to you? What do you value? To identify that takes some thought. Sometimes it also takes occasions where you see behaviour that is definitely not what you want. Remember, observe your kids, for they will reflect your values.

Values are the accepted principles or standards of an individual or group. They are the ideals you live by. They are measured by the time, effort and money you put into them. When something is of value to you, you will exchange your money for it. When looking around a market on a vacation, you will be exposed to many items which don't move you to part with your cash. Once you see that special something you will shell out the funds. Some people highly value their local football club. They buy the latest strip, text each other during games with the current score and spend astronomical sums on a season ticket. Why? In their eyes the team is worth it. The reason I mention the element of time, energy and finance in regard to values, is that some people will say they hold certain standards as values but their actions don't reflect it. The man who says his family is a value yet never spends any time with them is deluding himself.

Values are as diverse and as numerous as the individuals who hold them. You may value honesty, creativity, boldness, imagination, peace or curiosity. Often we aren't aware of what we value. Over time and from our family of origin, values are assimilated into our subconscious and we don't think about them until we are confronted with a situation that goes against the grain of our particular values. That's when you hear people say things like 'Oh, we don't hug in our family, or we never eat together.' Those are expressions of values you hold.

> WHAT YOU VALUE IS WHERE YOU PUT YOUR TIME, ENERGY AND MONEY.

One of the things we valued was a peaceful home. Something that contributed to that was lowered speaking voices. Bonnie would do this little thing with her hand where she would bring her fingers together with her thumb while saying 'small voice'. This is not to say our kids were quiet all the time. In fact our dinner table was extremely noisy. We only realised this after the twins left home and our youngest would be yelling at the table. It took a couple of months for her to realise that she didn't need to shout to be heard. Friends of ours didn't feel that this was important so everything their children said was at the top of their voices. But the parents were loud too. We shared a common wall between our houses and we were clearly entertained by everything they did. (Don't even think about that!)

Eating together was also a very high value for us. Having a family night together was the standard for quality bonding that was popular advice at the time our children were very young. That just didn't work for us. Our work often required that we be out in the evenings and it was impossible to get a consistent day of the week that was open. It also felt so artificial. We wanted to relate daily. So dinner became the priority. We would not answer the phone during that time. We blocked two hours of time for the meal. The whole family would share in the preparation and cleanup. We didn't clear up until after we had had a great time talking and laughing. Our children loved our meal times. One of their favourite things still is to invite friends over to experience mealtime with us. Sometimes it is overwhelming for their friends as the humour and jokes are non-stop. They still do this even now as young adults.

Humour and fun is an important value for us. My wife loves to laugh and has one of the most robust laughs you will ever hear. I can usually find her in any crowd by following the sound of her laugh. Watching comedy movies was always high on our list of quality family bonding activities. Quoting them in the midst of dinner conversations is a ritual peculiar to our little clan. Some people think we are just weird which is ok, as we think some of their values are weird. In fact most people think that what they value is what is truly important and those who do not value the same things are strange.

When you start your family you don't know exactly what you want. Usually Christmas brings the first distinct clarification of values. Often being torn between families and the disruption of routine causes you to decide you will stay at home and develop your own traditions. During Bonnie's first pregnancy, we spent Christmas with her family, which included our first nephew. He was six years old. Because his grandparents and aunts and uncles were there, he got a huge amount of presents. He had every conceivable gift possible for a little boy that year. At the end of this massive gluttony of gift opening he stood with his hands on his hips and declared, "Is that all there is?" When we got a chance to be alone we decided that we would never have that happen with our children. When the twins were born, they were the first grandchildren on my side of the family. They too got a plethora (lots) of gifts. To prevent what we saw happen with our nephew and to help them enjoy their new toys we had them open one in the morning and one in the evening for several days before Christmas Day. That way they weren't overwhelmed and they also had time to play with their gift before the next one was given to them. They still had a lot when they got to Christmas but nothing like what happened on our first family Christmas with our nephew.

You need to talk to each other. Your values are one of the areas you need to talk about. If you don't, you will give the children mixed messages as to what is right and appropriate. If you are contradicting each other, you will build up tension and resentment in your own relationship. For your sake and that of your child you need to be in agreement. You also have to be open to explore what the values of your family of origin were and how they may or may not compliment the values of your spouse's family. You may discover that you want to embrace something completely different from what your parents did. The only way you can change a value is to talk about it, otherwise you will keep on keeping on with what you have always done.

We talked so often about what we wanted for the kids that we had complete unity of mind. I remember the twins asking me during their later teen years if they could do something. I said 'Have you asked your mother?' They said they had and she had given them her opinion with the caveat 'but ask your Dad'. So I told them what I thought of their request, to which they responded 'Oh, brother! It's word for word the same as Mum's response. This is unbelievable!'

It really wasn't unbelievable if you knew the amount of time Bonnie and I spent communicating about what was valuable to us. Your children are a gift. If you don't believe me ask someone who hasn't been able to have children. It is worth the time and effort spent discussing what is important to be imparted for their future equipping as adults. In the introduction to this chapter I said that your children would reflect your values. They will reflect the things that you put time and effort into. If you are not happy with what you see, then you have to give serious consideration to what you want them to reflect.

POINTS TO PONDER

1. What is truly important to you?

2. Can you name three of your values?

3. If you have a partner, then discuss your values together.

4. What do you want your children to reflect?

Walk the Talk 3

Have you ever been in a restaurant or shop and heard a haggard parent saying: "If you touch that, or if you don't sit down, I'm going to do something to correct you"? The correction is usually a threat of some description, aimed to instantly evoke an obedient response from their child. Instead the child ignores them and keeps on doing what they were doing before the threat. Or in some cases they increase their misguided behaviour. What do the parents do? Nothing! No action to back their words up. They usually just repeat some inane threat that the child completely ignores by continuing to do just exactly what he or she wants.

What is the problem? The problem is not the child, the problem is the parent. Idle threats with no consequences! In fact, if they heard someone else saying the things that they have just said, they would laugh at how ridiculous it sounds. The child knows that their Mummy or Daddy is not going to walk the talk. They have learned that their parent's yes is not a yes and their no does not mean no.

Why do parents do this? One reason they give is they are afraid of the consequences of correcting their child in public, in case someone reports them to social services as an unfit parent. There are a number of flaws in this argument. Firstly, if you don't teach your child to be obedient to your authority, they will most likely get you into a situation at some point in their life, where you will have to deal with the authorities regarding the appropriateness of their behaviour. Secondly, it is basically a mirror image of the lack of authority and respect that exists in the home. Thirdly, it shows a mistaken idea that obedience is acquired through physical punishment, such as a smack on the backside.

To cultivate obedience in your child you need to walk the talk. You need to act on your words and to do that consistently. Did I say consistently? Consistently! If you are inconsistent, you lose the effectiveness of what you are trying to accomplish. A child needs your consistency in saying what you will do and then doing it. If you are going to shape their behaviour and ultimately their attitudes, you will only do it through consistently backing up your words with action.

Do you know what the problem is with this advice? The problem is that establishing consistency requires that you act when it is inconvenient

ACT ON YOUR WORDS AND DO IT CONSISTENTLY

and uncomfortable. You have a friend over for coffee and little Lily is drawing on the wall with a crayon. You say, "Stop that or I'll throw the crayons in the bin." Oops! Did you say that? You thought that the gravity of that threat might convince her to stop. The problem with this kind of threat is that it is unrealistic, punishing both you and your child. If you are going to make your word true, you have to throw a whole box of crayons in the bin. That costs you financially because you will want to replace them later. It costs you the inconvenience, as you will have to go to a store to buy them. It costs you in that your child can no longer do something they may really enjoy and that is a quiet, often solitary, activity. In your child's eyes it is a very extreme response in relation to what she were doing. It could even be viewed as hurtful in that you are taking such drastic action. This kind of statement really creates a 'no win' situation for you. If you don't follow through, you lose. If you do, you lose.

So your friend is over and you at last have a chance for some adult conversation, some time for yourself. You're right in the midst of a lovely conversation and Lily is drawing on the wall. I understand what it is like to just want to have some time for you. It will never come if you don't do something about it now. You need to sacrifice your pleasure now for a far more pleasurable future with your child. Get up from your coffee, walk over to Lily and say in a calm voice, "I don't want you to colour the wall, Lily." Take her back to the desk or table or spot where the colouring book is and tell her to colour there. Take action. Do not let it escalate until you are angry or she has done some great amount of damage.

Now we have done enough parenting seminars to know what you are thinking about what we have prescribed. You are thinking, "Right, like Lily is just going to nicely cooperate with me? So, now she is screaming and shouting and kicking her feet. What do I do with that? Seems to me this action has just escalated the problem." That may happen depending on what level of training your child is at. This will be dealt with in another chapter. The point of this chapter and the fundamental truth of parenting is to walk your talk. Do something to correct the behaviour and do it consistently day after day. This will produce an incredibly peaceful, well-behaved child. If you ignore this reality, their behaviour will get worse and you will not enjoy their childhood.

POINTS TO PONDER

1. Is there something that you unconsciously say to your child that is just an idle, unsubstantiated threat?

2. When are you most likely to ignore your child's behaviour?

3. Are you consistent in your words and actions?

4. What would be an appropriate response to undesirable behaviour that would create a win-win situation for you?

Whose Kid Is This?

When I was little I was convinced that my mother and father were aliens who had tied up my real parents and kept them captive in the attic. I was too short even with a kitchen chair to reach the cover to the opening of the attic. There my parents remained with all of us captives to these alien life forces. I was sure that my real mother and father would not be as strict as these people and would give me everything I wanted, if only I could get them free. Its funny how few people felt that way about their parents. I know, for every time I ask people about this at seminars, they just stare at me as if I'm the alien. There will be times when you will seriously wonder where this child of yours came from.

We forget that our children are people with real personalities right from conception. Just because they can't talk doesn't mean that

27

they are unaware of what is going on around them or of what they want. I have a university education and can speak English reasonably well, enough to be understood by the vast majority of English-speaking people I converse with. But in recent years we have had the privilege of spending time in France. Although I took six years of French in school, we never conversed in it. When I am in France, I am hopeless. I can't remember vocabulary, let alone pronounce words correctly. So even though I can't converse with someone in French, it does not mean I am unintelligent. I can still drive a car, watch videos in English and talk to my wife.

It is the same thing with a baby. Just because they can't talk, it doesn't mean they are unintelligent or unaware of what is going on around them. When Becky was 3 months old, Bonnie was having a real struggle to dress her. Every time she got one arm in and was working on the other, Becky would pull the first one out of the sleeve. Bonnie was totally frustrated. I suggested that Becky didn't want to wear a top and dungarees but a dress instead. Bonnie went ballistic. "She's only 3 months old! What would she know about clothes and the difference?" Taking my life in my hands I proposed that we present her with two choices, a dress and the dungarees. When we presented the dress, her face lit up. When we presented the dungarees, she made it clear she wasn't happy with them. (She had this little lip thing that she did when she wasn't happy. Her face turned red and her lower lip would stick out.) We clearly knew what she wanted and she was much happier when she got it.

Becky was very outgoing and confident. When we moved from our home where the twins had lived for three of their five years of life, Joel was very upset. He did not like the idea of leaving his friends. How would he meet new ones? "That's my problem," (which was his favourite saying). When we got to our new home, Becky took Joel by the hand and headed out, informing us that they were going to find some new friends. In a very short time they returned with a little girl their age that they had met at the house across the street. Soon a mother arrived with her son. She wanted to meet us and bring him to play.

> KNOW YOUR CHILD, FOR WHAT WORKS WITH ONE MAY NOT WITH OTHERS

Our neighbour told us that when she answered her door, Becky introduced Joel and herself, and then asked if they had any kids their age they could play with.

Becky's twin brother was more cautious and less assertive at times. He was very

29

sensitive and would respond to the first word of correction immediately, unlike Becky who we had to correct over and over and over for the same infraction. Even so, there would be times when he would go to do something and we would say "Joel" in the right tone of voice to stop him. You could see him weighing the decision. "Are the consequences of going for this worth it or not?" When he would disobey, he would get this little grin on his face.

Our youngest was very different from the first three, in that she knew exactly what she wanted. We would go into a fast food restaurant and she would tell me what she wanted and then head for the playground. The other three would hum and haw over their choices while the cashier waited patiently. Often to expedite things I would have to order for them. On one occasion we were helping Jess and her brother with their paper route. Jess asked if I would put a tissue in her coat pocket, as her hands were full with papers. Her coat had four pockets, two on each side. I went to put it in the top one closest to the side I was standing on. She told me, "Not there, that's my candy pocket". When I went for the lower one, she said, "No, that's my money pocket". She told me that her tissue pocket was the top one on the other side of the coat. So out of curiosity I asked what the bottom pocket on that side was for. She said that it was for anything interesting and worth keeping that she found on her travels.

One day as I was driving her to pick up a friend I asked her if she liked school. Having a very happy-go lucky disposition she told me, "Sure". It didn't sound too convincing. So I asked her if she really did. She said, "Daddy, you have to! It's the thing you have to do after the weekend." With this realisation of how she was feeling about school we scrutinised her situation more closely and made some changes so she would like school. Because she was a child that was willing to make the most of any situation, we could have left her to struggle on and end up hating education. One of the other clues was she did not want to have anything to do with university. It indicated that she was not enjoying what she was doing now, so why would she want to prolong this agony? I am happy to say that she really did enjoy the rest of her schooling after we made the changes.

The point is we need to know our children. What will work with one child won't work with another. One may need to be around people all the time to get their work done. Another may need time to be alone and to recover from being with people. You need to know who needs what. A situation can be totally restorative to one and totally stressful to another. Their behaviour will often reflect what they are feeling or how they are being treated.

By knowing them and allowing for their individual differences you can make their life and yours a whole lot more enjoyable.

There is nothing worse than being treated as if you were exactly the same as your brother or sister. When I was in my teens, my parents treated me as if I was exactly the same as my older brother. When I would ask to do something, they would say no, as my older brother had got himself into trouble doing that. It seemed to me that they never gave me the opportunity to prove otherwise. That led to a festering resentment that did lead to the kind of rebellious behaviour they were trying to avoid. It is so important to know your children and to treat them with appropriate respect for who they are.

POINTS TO PONDER

1. Do any of your children require time alone?

2. Are they intimidated by crowds or do they love being in the midst of the action?

3. What are children's likes and dislikes? Music? Athletics? Dance? Reading? Art? Hands on or observation?

4. Write a profile with 3 or more characteristics that best describe your child.

Somebody Praise Me

Have you ever noticed how adults will announce to everyone that they are going to use the toilet? It seems like a very strange thing for an adult to do. Why do we do that? We do it because it is a tremendous testimony to the power of praise and how effective it is in shaping behaviour.

Think about how we potty train children! We constantly encourage them to tell us if they need to use the potty. When they do, we praise them over and over again. When the children were little we used wine gums as a reward for using the potty, one for wee and two for, well, more. They thoroughly enjoyed the praise and the candy. In fact so much so that we had to start cutting the sweets in half so they wouldn't get too much sugar in one day. They used to carry the potty to us looking for the affirmation.

The evidence of the effectiveness of praise is demonstrated at every social gathering. Praise by its very nature is positive and people respond to positive input. Praise builds up and doesn't put down. Oh, how we all need to be encouraged!

Affirmation in the form of praise works well on any human being. I love it when my wife praises me. I have become such a glutton for it that I will some times say to her after a speech that I need, I need…. Tell me that I did well, please, please…. I didn't grow up with that level of praise and encouragement. I remember hearing only what I couldn't do or where I fell short. I could never excel enough to hear words of praise from my father. If I got 97 on an exam, the inevitable question was 'what happened to the other 3 marks?' I eventually gave up trying to succeed, as it was never good enough. When I married Bonnie, she encouraged me and told me I was great. I was uncomfortable with it at first because words like that were so foreign to me. But I soon started to like it and then started to believe it.

Praise for me was, as I said, foreign. So when I first started using it with our children, I felt awkward and stilted. But they didn't seem to notice. With perseverance praise became more and more natural. Don't say. "I can't do it," because you can. Don't say, "I won't do it because no one did it for me". Why punish your children for what you didn't have? Praise them! They will soon tell you how great you are. Praise your spouse and they will start to praise you as well. You reap what you sow. People tend to respond in kind. If you speak highly of them, they will of you. It is never too late to start encouraging someone and helping them to see and fulfil their potential.

In our marriage counselling we have met couples where one of them has nagged and nagged the other about something they wanted changed. The one suffering the nagging would confess that the nagging would just make them dig their heels in. Their back would go up and they would not change. The feeling one gets is: 'I can't do anything right so why try'. It becomes a personal assault on their self worth and creates insecurity as to your love for them. You said you loved me before and this wasn't an issue. Don't you love me now?

When our children were little we would use praise to support what we were teaching them to do. When they were between one and two years of age, we would help them pick up their toys and put them back in the toy box. As we did this together we would praise them for every toy they put in the box. "Wow, you're such a good boy! You did great putting that toy away. Wow, look at how many toys you've picked up! Isn't this great how quickly we can do this?" As they got better and better at doing this we continued praising and affirming their efforts but had to do less and less of the cleaning up ourselves. Eventually we could ask them to pick up their toys, which they would do by themselves. We would then praise and thank them for the great job they had done.

When they were four to five years of age, we would have them help us load and unload the dishwasher. The level of competency for any new task is low at the beginning. The cutlery made it into the drawer but not into the right tray. Instead of focussing on that, we praised them for helping and for putting it in the right drawer. As we went along we gave small corrections all the while praising them for what they were doing. Eventually we could ask them to do it and they would do it themselves. We would thank them and encourage them for helping out. We also wanted to acknowledge the importance of their contribution to the household.

Some people are concerned that if you praise your children all the time they will get a swollen head with pride. That, in essence, you are creating an arrogant human being. Praise gives you a wholesome sense of self-worth. Pride and arrogance comes from a lack of personal esteem and is a feeble effort to compensate for it. Society as a whole is negative and humour is often based on putting someone down. If your parents don't build you up in the home, where are you going to get it? If you do affirm and build up your children when they are young, they won't go looking for that affirmation somewhere else when they are older. They won't be looking for acceptance in gangs or in the arms of someone who is feeding that need for affirmation, to get what they want.

PRAISE YOUR
CHILDREN
DAILY

Praise creates an atmosphere that is full of love and acceptance. The person being praised feels loved and secure. It creates self worth and self esteem. Work at creating an atmosphere of praise in your house. Praise and affirm your family at every opportunity.

POINTS TO PONDER

1. Are you able to speak praise and encouragement easily?

2. What does your child do that you could praise them for? (List)

3. What are some worthy characteristics (like honesty, serving, compassion) of your child that you could praise? (List)

4. Have you praised them today?

Elementary, My Dear!

When we first got married, our television was not working properly. So I decided to try to fix it. As I was working patiently on the set my wife could sense that I was out of my depth. (I still don't know what gave me away.) She suggested that I hit it with the hammer. I was really puzzled about why she would give me this piece of advice. When I asked, she told me that her father fixed everything with a hammer. He had one solution for all problems.

It is important that as a parent you become a keen observer of human behaviour. If you don't, you will miss important clues to resolving what could end up being difficult situations. You will tend to have the same solution for every problem. What may work for one problem won't necessarily be the answer for another.

41

When our oldest son was 2 years old or so, he kept crying and crying and crying. We had done everything that we possibly could think of to try and get him to stop. Nothing was working. But by watching carefully we did notice him occasionally pull on his right ear. We decided to take him to the doctor to be checked. When they examined his ear, they said the eardrum was bright red and very infected. We felt like the world's worst parents under their scrutiny. One of the things that we learned from observing all our children is their incredibly high tolerance for pain. They certainly didn't get this from their father. Having once had an ear infection at the same time as they did, I ended up in bed whining while they were toddling around the house as if nothing was wrong. They were so tolerant of pain that none of them had words to describe a sore throat until they were in their teens. Armed with this information we were much more observant of anything that would give a clue to this kind of problem.

As children get older there are other things that can upset them and cause a reaction. What's been happening at school or on the bus? What is going on in the whole household can have an effect. Every time we moved they were upset. We used to have a beagle that always knew when we were going to our cottage, even before we started any of the packing. He would whine and whimper and generally get under our feet. Well children are just as intuitive as animals and they play up to get attention in those situations. Every time we moved their behaviour would be a pain in the lower extremities. It wasn't until we got wise to this phenomenon that we could do anything about it. We needed to talk to them and tell them what was going on. We needed to cuddle and hold them and reassure them of our love before they calmed down.

BE A KEEN OBSERVER OF YOUR CHILD'S BEHAVIOUR

Have you noticed that in the tensest situations your children start to get loud and start horsing around? On one trip through the Canadian Rockies our two youngest, then 10 and 12 years old were calm and collected through most of the drive. No fights, poking or fidgeting! But shortly after we got into a snowstorm where the wind was blowing the falling snow across the road at night they started to tickle and poke each other. They got louder and louder as the situation got more and more tense. So calmly I yelled my head off at them for making so much noise. After that my wife explained to them what a difficult situation we were in and I found the grace to apologise for my inappropriate response. I was forgiven which we will talk about later. The behaviour was not just them being kids, or being silly or bored. They were picking up on our tension and it stirred them up. Once they understood the situation they were fine.

Sometimes children act badly when they are tired. Why shouldn't they, we do? Your mind might be saying that they just got up so that can't possibly be tired. Yet, it can be. Remember they are growing and that alone can wear you out. Our daughter once had slept for 12 hours but was so cranky. She had been fed, changed, dressed and loved, yet was still crying and out of sorts. I suggested to my wife that maybe we should try bed. It seemed ridiculous after such a long sleep and the fact that she had only been up 2 hours. But when she was put to bed, she went fast asleep for another $2^{1/2}$ hours.

Make it a habit to process through all the possibilities if things aren't changing. Ask yourself what else this could be. Children have all the same responses as adults do in most situations but not necessarily the ability to react correctly. If a friend or colleague can embarrass us, our children can face much the same from a teacher or parent or friend. When I was teaching a class of nine and ten year olds, one of them finally said to me in total exasperation, 'Why do you embarrass me like that?' I was stunned. 'Like what?' I asked. He told me that he felt very embarrassed when I corrected him in front of the class. Up until then I had forgotten what it would feel like for me to be in that position. I had thought kids didn't react that way. But they do. From that point onward I determined to be more thoughtful of their feelings and how I would react in their place. They are, after all, sensitive, aware people.

One solution to all problems simply doesn't work. It may be the only one you use but it won't solve everything. I had the opportunity to work with my father-in-law on his air conditioner unit. Bonnie was right. He hit it with a hammer and then called an expert to come fix it.

POINTS TO PONDER

1. Is there a problem that your child is facing at the moment?

2. Has their behaviour changed in any way?

3. What do you see as the dynamics that could be disturbing your child?

4. What could you do to help?

Talk to Meeeee!

This may seem obvious but it is often lost in the busyness of parenting. Everything from exhaustion caused by too many early mornings, teething, through to extra-curricular activities collude to sabotage the most important thing in your relationship. After cuddles, feedings, baths, bedtime stories, laundry, your own dinner and cleaning up, it is possible to neglect talking to your spouse.

With the twins I arrived home to find everyone waiting for Daddy. No matter which one I chose they would fill their nappy for me. That led into the bath, then feeding and off to bed with a quick story, which kept getting longer as they got older. We chose the primitive method of cloth nappies, as we didn't think we earned enough to eat as well as buy disposables. I would carry down two buckets full of soiled nappies to the laundry in the basement where I would take one load out of the dryer, move the load in the washing machine over to the dryer, then put the two buckets of laundry into the washing machine, and finally take the basket full of clothes upstairs to the lounge where we would spend the next hour folding clothes and nappies. Somewhere along the line I would have turned on the TV and become absolutely mesmerised by some spellbinding thriller like a Charlie's Angels re-run. Trundling off to bed after completing the cycle we would hopefully sleep through the night so that we could do it all the same the next day.

Days can pass into years very quickly if you don't get a hold of this aspect of parenting. Maybe this is why some marriages end in divorce after the children leave home. If you haven't truly talked for the last twenty years, what could you possibly still have in common other than the children? Who is this other person you live with? In all likelihood you know your children better than your spouse.

You have to talk. For the sake of your own relationship now and in the future, you have to talk to one another. For your children's sake, you need to talk to each other. What good is it to be terrific parents and then separate when they are older? They want a relationship with you then too.

Talk for sanity's sake. The first and

second summers of our twin's lives my wife went back to summer school to finish her education degree. As I was a teacher I had the same time off so I thought it was a brilliant idea for me to care for the children while she completed her courses. It is very interesting being a father with the children in the park. Mothers, who make up by far the vast majority of adult people in playgrounds, do not talk to men, even when they have two babies with them. I was ostracised in the park and spent the whole day waiting for my wife to finish her classes. Why? So I could talk to an adult!!!! People, especially men, have mercy on your spouse if they have stayed with the children and talk to them when you come home.

TALK TO YOUR PARTNER OR A TRUSTED FRIEND FOR YOUR SANITY'S SAKE!

You also have to talk about what you are doing with your children. The key is to know what the other thinks about issues. Is that cute? Do you want them to suck their thumb or are you going to use a dummy? What about teething on the coffee table? Is that acceptable to you? Talking back – is that acceptable? Are you aware of how the baby is responding to me or to you?

Over the years we talked constantly about what we expected from our children, what was cute, what wasn't, schooling, behaviour, friendships, and whether our behaviour towards them was appropriate or not. We didn't always get it right the first time and needed to go back and correct what we had said. Sometimes we had to apologise for our own actions, as they weren't right. But we only knew it for sure because we talked to each other. We did not correct each other in front of the children as we felt this undermined the other's authority in the children's eyes. We wanted to honour the other person. Besides, we weren't always right in the way we perceived the situation either.

Well, what do you do if you are a single parent and don't have someone at home to bounce things off? I suggest you find a trusted friend who will listen to you and not be judgmental. It may be your parents who aren't as uptight now over things as they were when they had you, which can be good. Be aware however that something happens when you become grandparents where what was wise is now totally forgotten. Grandparents do things like feeding the children chocolate for lunch because they asked for it or jumping up and down with them until the kids are so wound up that they will never sleep. Also they sometimes go soft and don't think of what is really best for the children right now. So it may be wiser to ask a friend. People who are around us often can quite clearly see what is happening where we can't. Some times we have a blind spot that we need a little help with. If you enter into an agreement with a friend to get their perspective to help balance yours, I think you will find it very helpful.

You need to work at finding the time to talk. Take every opportunity. When the kids were small, we had evenings. As they got older, we took short walks or went out for coffee. You see builders don't start to build a house without plans. They lay the foundations from the blueprints they have before them. They have pictures of what the house will look like when it is completed. They keep referring to the plans throughout the entire process to make sure they get it right.

I had the opportunity in my short career in construction to give a quote on a roofing job for the general contractor. The builders had started some of the work when I arrived to quote from the plans. As I looked the plans over I became confused as to exactly where the rooflines joined on the blueprints. Because I was pretty green at this sort of thing, I called the contractor over and asked for his help. As we went over the plans he realised the architect had made a serious mistake and that the roof sections could not come together as drawn. He apologised and sent the plans back to the architect to be corrected.

If we need plans for something as basic as a house, how much more do we need to be actively planning and correcting the course of our children's lives? We have the responsibility for them for such a very short time. We are all products of our parents' efforts. If we want to be the best parents we can be for our children, then we need to talk.

POINTS TO PONDER

1. Do you have someone to talk to? If not, can you think of someone you could approach for his or her ear?

2. What are your expectations for your child/ children? (Jot them down in the space below).

3. Are you aware of areas of difficulty involving other people's children? Could you help them if they were open to your advice?

4. Would you be willing to have someone speak into your situation?

The Early Warning System

As your children become more mobile they become inquisitive and constantly reach for any object they can get close to. You can baby-proof your house by putting all the trinkets and things of value up high. But incredibly they will find something you missed. Besides hanging all your plants upside down from the ceiling isn't particularly good for their health. Loading the DVD player at that height is also difficult for anyone under six feet in height. The disks tend to fall out before you can get the tray back into the machine.

Where do all of the things go when they get their hands on them? In their mouth! That's right. Gross! We had one couple bring their 11-month-old daughter to the house for a visit. She proceeded to chew her way all the way around our wooden coffee table. The parents would either ignore her or tell her to stop in a jovial tone of voice. We sat there in amazement. Guess what became one of our toddler values? When the couple spoke to their daughter, they did not give her any tonal clues that she was to stop, nor did they take any action to stop her. There were two issues in this situation that needed to be addressed. One was the issue of appropriateness of her actions, and the other was the issue of what the varnish was made of. In the good old days paints were lead-based. What our table was varnished with was anybody's guess.

You need to be prepared to act on the basis of these two criteria: appropriateness and safety. You don't want your children destroying property because they ignore your words. You also don't want them to hurt themselves because they ignored your words. But if you are always talking at them and never taking action, they just hear noise coming at them. Always talking at your child will make you upset and irritable because they don't respond. I remember saying to Bonnie, "I'm getting worn out saying the same thing over and over again. I'm also getting mad and this isn't good".

> USE A WARNING SYSTEM AND BE PREPARED TO RESPOND IF YOUR CHILD DOESN'T

As a result of this, we developed what

we called our early warning system. We decided that one warning to stop was not enough. To correct their behaviour on one warning did not give enough time for them to hear, assimilate and respond. We decided two warnings gave them a sense of the gravity of the situation but still time to react. So we settled on three warnings as the point of action on our part. They had heard, they had time to respond and hadn't, so now was our time to do something.

We would say, 'Jared, put that down.' If he didn't I would say 'one' and give him a chance to respond. If no response, I would say two. Again no response I would say three. If at that point he had not done what I had told him, I would go to him and either remove him from what he was doing or take the object away from him. If he started to cry, I would put him in his cot or playpen or give him a book.

I did not fill the space between numbers with words. I wanted Jared to know the countdown was on. I also didn't want to get upset by saying things that he didn't respond to. At three I would start to rise so he knew I was coming. I didn't rise in anger. It's not anger you want them to respond to. It's consistency! Consistency creates the appropriate response. Of course it takes time for them to realise you will act on 'three' but once it is learned they respond to your warnings.

We are also not talking about emergency situations such as the child is playing in the road with a car approaching. Then you simply act as fast as possible. We are talking about the model airplane that their older brother has laboured lovingly over that they have just picked up. You say 'No! Put it down! 1...2... (Rising as you say) 3.'

I have heard people try this but make the mistake of saying things in-between. Maybe they don't want to get up or maybe they don't really think its that serious. But saying '1..Don't make me come over there...(long pause) I said don't do that...2....Johnny don't do that. Stop or I'll ground you from TV for a week....3....Don't make me come over there...Alright then.' And then they get up. The child knows that in reality your warning system is not three but at least ten. It is fascinating to watch children who know that. They will stop just before the parent gets up.

All the time that is wasted is incredible. Whatever you were doing has been put on hold for all that time, whether conversing with someone or preparing food. It all has to wait through the entire duration of this process.

We didn't start this process during the first years of life with the twins. We began doing this around the age of three. Because we hadn't done this earlier we explained the early warning system to them before we started using it. They needed to know in advance what we were going to implement. This eliminated confusion on their part. The first few times we said, 'Remember what Daddy and Mummy said we were going to do? Put that toy away.... 1....2....(rising)3.' Guess what? We had to go to three every time for the first week or so. Why? Because the system was new to them and they needed to know that it was actually what we meant. With our next baby, Jared, we started the system as soon as he was mobile enough to get into things. That mobility came at between 6 and 7 months when he started to move his walker around. We would even leave something within his reach to teach him the early warning system.

Often the children would make us go to 3 and some times they wouldn't respond at all. Did we give up using it then? No, we got up and took the item away or moved them. If they threw a tantrum, we did not stand there discussing it with them. We dealt with the tantrum with the appropriate action.

What you are developing is obedience to your word. You want them to internalise that it is important to obey Mummy or Daddy. In the case of a dangerous situation you want to be able to call out 'NO or STOP' and have them obey immediately.

Ultimately the early warning system has

a two-fold purpose. One is to teach your child to obey what you say. The other is to eliminate your growing frustration and anger with your own children. If you spend years and years chasing after disobedient children, you will grow to dislike the very person who most needs your support and affection. All through this book we are giving you principles and practices that will not only help you develop wonderful children but will also give you a real joy in having children.

POINTS TO PONDER

1. Do you have a warning system in effect?

2. Do you need to implement such a system?

3. Do you talk too much at your children?

4. Do you find yourself frustrated with and resentful towards your children?

What Are We Going to Do Tonight?

"Bonnie, will you marry me so that we can have children?"

"Why of course darling! Nothing could make me happier than marrying you and having your children." And so they lived happily ever after in their house filled with children. Well... until they all grew up and left home that is.

When I proposed to the most beautiful girl in the whole world, I wasn't thinking about children. I had found the girl who I loved passionately and wanted to spend the rest of my life waking up next to every morning. After a few years we started thinking about having children. Our children are now all adults and at the time of writing we are looking at 25 years or more together just the two of us. That's as long as we had the children with us. So how do you preserve that which you started with? By considering the advice that follows.

Here it is: keep a date night once a week. When we had the twins, Bonnie's parents gave us that advice. They said a date, not a group meeting or some work-related activity. Get a babysitter and make it a priority. Not normally one to take advice when I was young, I, for once, did agree. (Funny in light of the fact that we are now writing a book giving people advice.) From the twins third month on we followed this rule.

I know what you're thinking. Yes, it is costly. Yes, it is also tough to find someone trustworthy to leave the children with. But the amazing fact is that people can always find money for the things that they put a high value on. I have known couples with very limited resources that would spend huge amounts of money on musical instruments. Somehow they could afford them because the value they received from the instruments was more than the value they held for the cash.

When you are having children, your friends are usually in the same boat as you. T o help with the babysitting costs we used to take care of our friends' children and they ours. It isn't too difficult when they are all in bed.

Not only are you showing high value to one another but you are also teaching your children how to love and respect a future spouse. You entered into this relationship for each other. Children are the fruit of your relationship not the desired goal of it. After they are older you will appreciate the money as well spent.

Well, what do you do if you are single? Book a babysitter once a week and go out with one or more friends. You need a life outside of the children too. You get to breathe fresh air and talk to someone about something more than 'Bob the Builder'. You'll feel better after some time out and that will help you be a better parent.

What do you do for the evening? You do whatever you find refreshing for you and your partner. We loved to go to dinner at a quiet restaurant and talk. We have friends who enrolled in a ceramics class together. They sat next to each other at the workbench and found that romantic. Our daughter and her spouse tend to go to the cinema. Do whatever you enjoy and find revitalising.

> TAKE A BREAK WITHOUT YOUR CHILDREN FOR YOUR SAKE AND THEIRS

Try to talk about something other than the children, although some shoptalk is inevitable. Make sure it is something that leaves you feeling refreshed and mentally stimulated. The one who is going to work outside the home may not feel the need for extra stimulation. But the one who has been the main caregiver will definitely need the time to have their mental capacities stimulated. To keep the love burning in your relationship take the time to stoke the fire.

POINTS TO PONDER

1. Do you ever get out of the house without the children?

2. What would you enjoy doing during your time out?

3. Is there someone you could exchange babysitting duties with?

4. Why is it a good idea to go out?

In Cold Blood

When we share these principles it is not only for your children to behave better but it is also for your peace of mind. Having fully experienced parenthood we know the fears and concerns parents have. You want to enjoy your children. You want them to enjoy you. You don't want to do some of the things you experienced with your own parents. So you may over-compensate where you thought your parents were wrong, harsh or over-reactive. You may feel that you should just be able to speak to your children and everything will work out fine. Then as you go along and your child ignores you, you feel all kinds of emotions that you never wanted to feel towards them.

You may have experienced talking to your child about something over and over and over again until you become angry. Then in

69

anger you have punished them. You then feel guilty because you over-reacted out of anger. You determine you won't do that again. Trying patiently to maintain your cool, you find the same cycle recurring with your child and then you react in anger. The guilt increases and you seem caught in an ever- increasing cycle of anger and frustration. Maybe you chose the route to simply ignore the behaviour and opt out of trying at all to bring correction. Unfortunately the no correction choice has eventual results that you and your child will probably regret. It also says to them that you don't love them because you don't set boundaries or enforce them. That creates within your child insecurity and a feeling of not being loved.

I can remember that the times I resented my parents were when they punished me unjustly. It was over the top and I didn't feel I deserved it. One time I was about 11 playing outside in the snow when I got involved in a situation with the neighbour's kid who was about 6 years old. He had this fantastic mound of snow in his garden that they had dug a tunnel through. I wanted to go through it but he and his friend were having no part of it. As a bigger kid, I figured that if I threatened to break the tunnel he would capitulate and let me crawl through. Instead he went wild, attacking me with his fists swinging. As I was trying to stop him, my mother who saw this from the kitchen window, came out on the steps and told me to leave him alone and come home right now. He was all over me and I was trying not to hurt him or his fort, I had just made an idle threat, which I had no intention of carrying out. She continued to call me home with more and more emphasis and consequences if I didn't respond. In frustration I told my mother to shut up. I extricated myself from the situation without any damage to kid or fort and went home as told. I was then sent to the basement to wait for the inevitable spanking that would come with my father's return from work.

The spanking I received burned more than my backside. I was indignant that my mother assumed the worst of me and made demands of me that were creating a worse situation than before. Yes, I suppose I spoke wrongly but there was no room for any apology or explanation as to why I spoke as I did. It was this kind of incident that burned into my memory. It was the correction out of anger that created resentment in me. When they calmly went about the business of correcting me, I understood that I deserved it. When my parents were angry, it scared me and seemed way out of proportion to what I was doing.

In light of this, consistency of action

with a measured response is important. I used to call it acting in cold blood. You are setting limits so you will not lose your temper. You need to respond to your children's behaviour calmly. You need to act on your values and what you have decided together. You need to do it before you have been pushed to anger. We would try to consistently act while we were calm, cool and collected. One of us would say something like 'Do we want him doing that?' If the reply was no, we addressed the situation.

Have I always stayed calm? No. I wish I could say I had. When I blew it, and usually I knew I had in the midst of it, Bonnie and I would talk about it without the kids around. If she concurred that it was inappropriate, I would go back to the kids and say I was sorry. I would probably explain what I saw them doing wrong but I would also explain that I acted wrongly too. I would tell them I was sorry and ask them to forgive me. We would always have them say 'I forgive you' rather than 'that's ok'. Why? It wasn't ok, or I wouldn't be apologising.

CONSISTENTLY ACT WITH A MEASURED, CALM RESPONSE

Does this show weakness? Not if you were wrong. It eliminates the resentment for being harshly or unjustly punished. It gives credence to when you do correct them as being fair and just. They know you aren't perfect, they will only resent it when you pretend you are.

Training your children consistently and in cold blood will keep your stress levels down. It will save you apologising or losing faith with your child. You will not have all the detrimental physical effects upon your body that anger brings. Overall you will be a much happier person.

POINTS TO PONDER

1. Do you discipline your children in cold blood?

2. Do you wait until you are angry or frustrated?

3. What changes can you make to achieve the desired behaviour?

4. Can you write out your plan so you have it on hand for the next encounter?

I'm Sorry

We met a woman a number of years ago who shared with us an incident that happened when she was five. Her older sister and she fought over her sister's new red wagon. There was so much antagonism and subsequent resentment towards her sister that they had hardly talked or related to each other from that point on. What a shame! 20 years of friendship wasted all due to an inability to forgive. She had at the time of our meeting just recently forgiven her sister and renewed contact with her. It was the beginning of the healing and restoration of their relationship, but there would always be the sorrow of regret for the years lost.

'I'm sorry' are very powerful words. Even more than 'you've got mail'. (My wife's favourite movie) Forgiveness is essential to the wholeness and wellness of everyone in the family. Parents need to forgive the kids, the kids need to forgive the parents, and the kids need to forgive each other. We started right from before they could speak, telling them we forgave them or acknowledging that they were sorry.

Being a keen observer of people, I have witnessed sibling after sibling relationship where they resent each other. It is a situation where they love each other but they don't like each other. If incidents happen time after time where there is no resolve, resentment festers. Children have an incredibly keen sense of justice, of what is right and what is wrong. They very much want the law to be in their favour all the time and ignored when they are wrong.

Saying "I forgive you" does not mean that what the other person did was right. It simply means that you release them from the wrong they have done, or you perceive them to have done, and you won't hold it against them. Children need to be taught how to forgive; it is not natural or innate.

It is also not an issue of how you feel. You will never feel like forgiving. Forgiveness is a decision of the will. Your feelings will respond to whether you chose to forgive or not. Having taught the children to seek and give forgiveness, we have had some occasions where they have done something really wrong, like Joel cutting a 6" chunk out of the back of Becky's hair. They have asked us to forgive them, which we have done. But we have had to ask them to leave the room for we are still mad and don't want to react while in that state of mind. In a few minutes we are usually calm and ready to interact. We just needed the space.

As I have written in another chapter of the book, we, as parents, have asked the children to forgive us where we were wrong. This brings an incredible healing into relationships. As they get older the issues change from 'it's my toy' to interpersonal actions. When Jess was looking to take her 'A' Levels, she wanted to be a teacher. I was not in favour of it. I had been a teacher, knew what students and parents were like and saw no reason for my daughter to put herself through that. I actively dissuaded her. I encouraged her to take journalism or creative writing, anything but teaching. Finally I realised that I could be robbing her of the opportunity to fulfil her destiny, the one thing she was made for. So I asked her to forgive me and told her she had my blessing to be a teacher. You know what she decided after I had humbled myself? She decided she wouldn't be a teacher after all.

Hello! What was that about? I kept looking for Bonnie to give me some explanation, you know, with women being from Venus and men from Mars. I thought a woman would understand. She didn't. Recently Jess has decided that she will qualify as a teacher after she finishes her degree. She changed her mind again. Right, it's a woman's right to change her mind.

If our children learn to forgive in the family, they will also apply it to relationships outside the home. Remember the old saying 'sticks and stones may break my bones but names will never hurt me'. It is such a lie. When we came home from school upset by the teasing that happened, we probably all were taught that prosaic verse by our parents. I never did accept it. Names wound far deeper than stones and won't heal unless one learns to forgive. One time Joel, then 5, came home very upset with one of the boys in the neighbourhood. He had actually been arguing with one of the boys about the existence of angels. Carl (not his real name) joined in and taunted Joel about it more than the first boy. Joel told us he said to them 'angels are real' then punched Carl hard in the stomach. After we consoled him and reassured him of our belief in angels too we explained that you couldn't make someone believe by force. I took him to see Carl to apologise for punching him. Both Carl and his father were equally stunned to have Joel and I apologise for the punch. They both forgave him and we went away happy.

FORGIVENESS IS ESSENTIAL AND VERY POWERFUL

When the kids were small, if they bit the other one or took their toy or something else along these lines, we would have them say to the offended one 'I'm sorry.' Then we would have the other child say 'I forgive you.' Then we would have them hug. You might think that they would resist this but they actually expected it to happen.

A lack of forgiveness, as we can see by the example at the beginning of the chapter, can foster separation and deep-seated resentment within siblings. It can cause your child to disrespect you if you fail to respond in situations where you were wrong. It can also cause you to carry resentment towards your children. Parents have told me that they find one of their kids so much easier to love than another. The reason? They are carrying resentment towards the child when they should forgive them.

Did we have a house totally free of conflict? No! There were six people living in one house together. People will inevitably have conflict with one another. Learning how to deal with the conflict removes its lasting effects. Forgiveness creates harmony in the home.

POINTS TO PONDER

1. Do you forgive easily?

2. What angers you the most?

3. Do you feel resentment towards your children?

4. Try practising speaking forgiveness out loud. Think of an incident where you could apply forgiveness. Now speak out these powerful words: "I forgive you _____ for _____."

Start Early

When the twins were three we met a couple that had a two year old and a one year old. At the time we were seriously considering having another child. Visiting them set our baby back two years. The mother was letting her baby feed herself. Everything was covered with dried on blended baby food. You know how it always has those sensual colours: browns, greens and oranges. It was caked to the wall behind her highchair, to the chair, to the floor and to the table. In fact you could find samples of it nearly anywhere in the room that she could flick it to with a spoon.

This eventually prompted a conversation about the virtues of not allowing a baby to feed itself all the time, which further led to a discussion about the ability of the baby to comprehend language. The mother was convinced that she just didn't understand words like 'no' or 'don't touch'. She thought that she was just a little baby with no ability to think or understand. (This was the same logic that led to allowing the child to feed itself from the time she was nine months old).

We asked the mother to try a little experiment to see if her baby understood language or not. After hosing her baby down from the feeding trough, we asked her to put baby on one side of the lounge with her toys. Then to sit on the other side, call the baby by name and if baby turned to her, ask her to come and give Mummy a big hug. Much to her surprise, the baby turned at her name, then immediately toddled over and threw her arms around Mummy. Mummy was amazed initially, then very pleased when she realised how much her baby understood. Up until then the child wouldn't do anything she said, so she assumed she didn't understand.

We have given you examples of Becky when she was three months, of this baby at twelve months and our son in his walker at seven months. All of them showed clearly that they are intelligent and learning more every second of the day. They have a personality when they are born that you get the glorious opportunity to shape through their childhood. You need to start early.

When Jared was 8 months old, he was getting very demanding in his attitude. I knew a showdown was coming. I had had one with Joel when he was very young. Jared was not happy and wanted his way. During his nap Bonnie took the other two to swimming lessons. I was to wait for him to wake, and then go to the pool to get Joel, and take him to football (soccer). I told her I might be late as it looked as though a temper time show down had arrived.

When Jared woke up, he was not happy. He wasn't happy having his nappy changed. He wasn't happy with his bottle. He was angry and started to cry the mad cry. I said to him that he wasn't going to win and let him cry. After a very deafening period of time, he stopped. I asked Jared if it was over and could we go now? He didn't cry anymore so we went off to the game, as we were late for the pool pick-up. From that point on he was very happy and we usually only had to say his name once when he was doing something wrong to get him to stop.

START EARLY TO SHAPE THEIR PERSONALITY

Bonnie described it as a very deliberate clash of wills. You see it all the time in public places where the child wants something and throws a tantrum to get it. What you are witnessing is a toddler ruling the household. I knew a couple that told their two-year-old son to turn out the light when he went to bed. They would go to bed before him. How dangerous is that? They said there was just nothing they could do with him so they had given in to letting him have his way in all things.

The sooner you start the easier it will be. All training must obviously be age appropriate. The goal of all your efforts is to internalise the values and/or practices that you think are important for your children's development. This takes repetition and consistency. For example, brushing their teeth before going to bed. We brushed their teeth for them until they were able to do it well themselves. Every night when they would be ready to go to bed, we would ask them if they had brushed their teeth. They would say no and we would send them back to the bathroom to brush them. This went on until they were nearly teens. But one day they got it and we never had to ask them again. Another is boys and showers. Until they are teenagers, boys will never think of having a shower. They will go to great lengths to avoid it. But suddenly something happens at around 13 and you can't get them out of the bathroom. In fact they become worse than the girls for primping.

What you are doing as a parent is preparing your children to become well-adjusted adults. You are consistently reinforcing values and appropriate behaviour until it becomes a part of them. You continue until they no longer need to be told, they just do it. The earlier you start the better behaved your children will be. But remember it is never too late to start!

POINTS TO PONDER

1. Who rules in your house?

2. What could you do to make a difference to your child's obedience?

3. What values do you want your child to internalise?

4. How are you going to make it happen?

Choices

All of us like to have the option to choose what we want. In restaurants we often want to make slight changes to menu items so they are just the way we want them. We ask for our apple tart to come with maple walnut ice cream instead of vanilla. Most restaurants will accommodate slight alterations, although our German friends said the waiter will listen to you in Germany and then bring you what is set on the menu anyway!

Children are no different than adults. They want to have a say. It is wise to use this desire as a way of securing their cooperation around the home. We would find that when we asked the kids to go outside, they would say no. The first word used by all two year olds to exert their will. We would give them a choice of what they would like to do. The key is making the choices acceptable activities for you. We would say ' Would you like to go outside or upstairs for a nap?' They would say 'Hmm! Outside.' 'Good choice, let's get your boots and coat on.' They would be much more cooperative in getting ready as they had decided to go outside.

GIVE YOUR CHILD THE OPPORTUNITY TO CHOOSE FROM WISELY DETERMINED CHOICES

You can use it with things like wearing a hat. 'Do you want to wear the blue hat or the flowered hat?' They then feel some level of control in their life. 'I chose this.' When you take them to a restaurant, say, 'what would you like for your meal: the hamburger, cheeseburger or chicken?' In some cases they might even want to be empowered to the point of extra pickles or no pickles.

Give your children every opportunity to make choices. Look for situations where they can say what they want so that you can elicit their cooperation. Remember there are some areas where you must be the one who decides what they are doing. Don't abdicate that responsibility too soon. As they get older they will want to be involved in decisions involving their education. You are guiding them to make right choices as they grow.

We would include the children in having an opinion on the car that we were purchasing. On one vehicle purchase we were all in agreement on the type of vehicle that we needed as a family. Because of the dilapidated state of our existing car we needed to make the change in the middle of a trip of about 1200 miles. We were going from one dealership to another looking for an available people mover. We found one that was two tones of grey. All of us thought it was great except Joel. He didn't like the colour; he liked the one we had seen in the city 350 miles behind us. I had to explain to him that we didn't have much option on colour as this was the only one available and I seriously didn't think we would be able to drive our own car off the sales lot. (We had driven the last 30 miles with the alternator light on, the heater off, no radio or anything that would use more power. It was about 20 degrees below outside. So he knew the condition of the car.) Joel accepted this and with the family in agreement I proceeded with negotiations. Interestingly, he was fondly remembering that car a couple of months before this writing. Even though it wasn't his initial choice, he knew that he had been included and his opinion heard.

Some of the greatest frustration for people, adults and children alike is the feeling that you weren't heard in the decision-making process. You feel that things are foisted upon you in which you had absolutely no say. You had concerns that weren't heard, let alone considered. This is especially difficult to swallow when the decision turns out to be wrong.

When the twins were approaching their thirteenth birthday, we decided it was time to switch gears from parties to more mature celebrations. We decided we would take them to very nice restaurants. The reasoning behind this was to provide them with experience in the area of higher quality dining, in preparation for when they started to date. It was also great for us. They chose the restaurant too. We did this with all the children. We have on occasion thrown them a surprise birthday party after the dinner. Inevitably giving them choices leads to expense as they have all chosen the most expensive item on the menu. At this point you grin and bear it. It was my idea, anyway.

When children are young, choices are very effective in procuring their cooperation around the house. Choices empower them while eliminating a great deal of the struggle of wills between parent and child.

It reduces much of the tension that exists when you are trying to get them to do what you want. As they get older the choices will get more complex. You need to engage them in giving a reason why they would choose that. As with Joel and the car, he was able to express that it was only the colour that he wasn't in favour of. If children haven't had the opportunity to make choices, they will flounder when it is important. They will go with the crowd rather than make a choice that is contrary. If they are used to choosing and having to think through why this choice, they will be much stronger in decision-making when they are on their own. Our kids would often choose not to watch movies at friends' homes, as they knew that some types disturbed them. They would either come home or call for a lift.

What do you do if you haven't done this up until now? Well, start giving them opportunities to make small choices between two options, either of which you are happy with. Don't overwhelm them by throwing them completely into the deep end. Start with one decision a day, then gradually increase the number of choices they have. Talk to them about why they chose that one instead of the other. Give them feedback on the options so that they learn to think through the results of their choices. Don't say to them that their choice was a bad choice. Remember you are supplying the options so either choice should be good. Criticising their choices will only make them totally resistant to any suggested change. Honour their choices and encourage them to chose well. Ask them if they were happy with their choice afterwards so that they will think through the effects of it. To do this, ask them simple questions like 'would you chose that again? Why or why not?'

Your children will be faced with choices all their lives. The best place to learn is in the home. It is such an essential part of life that children start asserting their will to chose virtually from birth. Rather than fight it, mould it through guided choices.

POINTS TO PONDER

1. Do you give your child choice options?

2. Can you describe situations where it would be good for your child to have a choice?

3. Are there situations when you have felt your opinion wasn't being heard?

4. Can you visualise your child making good choices and you being able to discuss it with them?

.

Garbage In, Garbage Out

What you watch has a profound effect on you. I watched a movie on TV with my parents when I was about ten that had one murder scene. The scene was filmed so that you knew the murderer had knocked his victim down and smashed his head in with a rock. Gruesome! It gave me nightmares. I can still see it in my mind's eye. Bonnie saw the movie, The Blob, when she was about ten and she had nightmares too.

This is a common experience. We took the kids to see Honey, I Shrunk the Kids on the encouragement of some close friends who had grown-up children. They loved it and thought our kids would too. Jared, aged 5, stood through the whole movie and would often hold onto my leg for security. Jessie, aged 3, sat on Bonnie's lap with her face buried in Bonnie's chest. At the end of the movie she held Bonnie's face in both of her wee hands, looked her directly in the eye and said 'don't you ever take me to a movie like that again'.

For her and Jared the movie was reality. There was no fantasy, they were not old enough to distinguish between that and reality. To them it wasn't a comedy but a horror film. Who would purposefully take their children to a horror film? Yet children may feel exposed to the same effects as if they had gone to one. I have seen children 5 or 6 years of age in The Lion, The Witch and the Wardrobe. They and their parents spent a lot of time going to the toilet during the movie.

We need to fully grasp the gravity that what our children watch will deeply affect them. We have to take the responsibility to monitor what they watch on TV. Just because it is labelled a child's program does not mean the content is suitable. We found that when the twins watched an extremely popular American daytime show with unusually different creatures and characters they became hyper. They would be so wound up; they would just fly around the house. If that fits in with your values, then you will have no problem with the show. For us it didn't. We wanted peaceful children, not ones bouncing off the walls. We could not initially figure out what was stirring them up so much. We narrowed the timing down to it happening after this show. So we tried watching it. It was a complete assault on the senses with numbers flashing in and out and whirling around with a barrage of sound to accompany it. We couldn't take it ourselves and turned it off. From that point on the twins did not watch it. Amazingly, they did learn their numbers and letters before they went to school without the assistance of that particular show.

Remember each child is different. Joel was very perceptive and sensitive. One day he ran into the lounge from watching the Flintstones and hurled himself on the couch sobbing. We were very startled. We asked what was wrong. He said, 'Oh, that Fred, he's so mean to Betty. He lies to her all the time and gets away with it'. We thought the Flintstones! So we watched a show. Joel was right, Fred did tell lies to Betty, to Barney and to his boss, Mr. Rubble. And some how he always managed to get away with it. For Joel this was very disturbing. Becky sat through the whole thing without a care or concern. Two of our kids were very aware of the material in shows and would turn them off. The other two appeared brain dead when it came to shows and would watch anything. These ones we had to supervise closely and monitor what they looked at. We would engage their minds through questions to get them to think about what they were watching, eventually asking them if they thought this was an appropriate show for them. They would often agree and change to another programme.

As they moved into their teens we started watching movies rated above a U with them. We would rent 2 movies. One that was a U rating that we could all watch and one that was a higher rating, usually PG. (These rating have constantly changed through the last 20 years so you need to decide what rating to start with.) One of us would watch the movie before we viewed it as a family. If we felt it was acceptable then we showed it, otherwise we got another movie. (And people wonder how I've come to watch so many movies) We would then talk to the kids about the theme of the movie. We'd ask them what they thought of it, why they liked it, what was it about, what was the director or author trying to tell us? Any question that would effectively launch a discussion would do. We wanted them to be able to determine what made a good film vs. a bad one. We also didn't want them to go from totally sheltered to total freedom without gradual guided steps. Many scenes we would fast forward if they were inappropriate. We have joked with the kids that they will expect sex to be a very fast activity.

One of our friends grew up in a very religious home that did not allow TV, comics or movies. His Saturday morning chore was to get the paper before the other kids, remove the comics and destroy them. He had absolutely no ability as an adult to discern between what were and weren't appropriate TV shows or movies. He watched them all. On top of that he watched many of them with his 3 and 5-year-old sons. If his wife complained, he told her not to be ridiculous, that it was fine. Often when children have been unable to do things they swing to the other extreme as adults. So his parents were worried about garbage in but created an adult who had no ability to discriminate, in fact, felt deprived and was making up for lost time.

BE AWARE THAT WHAT YOUR CHILDREN WATCH WILL AFFECT THEM

The role as a parent is to educate your child. You need to determine what is safe for them to watch and to gradually develop their ability to discriminate as they mature. We don't automatically have this ability. It takes someone to teach us.

POINTS TO PONDER

1. Have you ever watched a movie that disturbed you?

2. Do you know what your children are watching on TV and on the Internet?

3. Are your children having bad dreams or exhibiting behaviour that you don't want?

4. Do you use TV as a babysitter? How much TV do your children watch? How much time do they spend on the Internet?

The Art of Conversation

Words are learned. The ones repeated to us the most are the ones we learn first. 'Mummy, Daddy and no' seem to rank right up there as the most repeated words. As we have stated in other parts of the book, children very quickly get a basic grasp of language and can respond before they talk.

But words do need to be taught. We forget this and often tell our children to do things that they just don't understand. Have you ever picked up toys with your toddler and you say, 'Get the one behind you', and they don't. In fact they seem somewhat mystified as to what you have just asked them. They may stand up and look in front of them but not behind. At that point it appears that they are just being disobedient and that could frustrate you. The conclusion you may come to is they don't want to do it. The reality is they don't understand your words. You need to teach them the meaning.

We did this with every child. At the table we would ask them questions like 'Who is across from you? Who is beside you? What is behind you?' When they didn't know we would tell them the answer and explain the word to them. The next day we would play the game at the dinner table again. Repetition establishes the understanding and use of the word.

To have conversations you need to help your children acquire a vocabulary. Reading to them is essential. Ask them questions during or after the story. If there was a word they didn't understand you could define it for them. Leave books in their cot or bed and around the house so they find words as natural a part of life as breathing.

Throughout this book we constantly refer to talking to your children and having a conversation, for example about a movie. Some of you who are reading this probably think 'Right, a conversation. Not going to happen!' You know your children. They come home from school and you ask them 'How was school?' 'Fine.' What did you do in class? 'Nothing!' Who did you play with? 'No one.' Any homework? 'Nope.'

Now here you have a book where the authors advocate talking to your children. You may not have received any more than monosyllabic responses from them from the time they started school. It doesn't make sense in the light of the fact that they are supposed to be getting educated. There are different reports every so often of how little time a child spends in conversation with an adult during a day. I've heard different lengths of time but definitely nothing over 15 minutes. That includes all conversation from 'Mum, Billy took my hair brush' to 'Nope' after school to 'Do I have to' after dinner.

Our children were no different. One of our main practices after they started school was dinner together. We wanted to stay connected on a daily basis. So "Nope" or "Nothing" was not going to work as stimulating dinner conversation. We would ask them the usual questions about school, which got the usual answers. I still distinctly remember saying: 'All right. Tell me what you did when you got to school. Did you go in right away? No, well what did you do? Then who did you talk to? What was your first class? What were you working on?'

I still don't know why they only call the delivery of a baby "labour". It's all hard work, especially developing their ability to hold a conversation. We agonised through the process every single night until they got better at being forthcoming with information. You have to persevere. I think initially they don't know what to say. When they get a little older, I think they wonder if you are really interested. So stay interested and pursue them. Make your questions as open ended as possible so they

DEVELOP THE ABILITY TO CONVERSE THROUGH ASKING YOUR CHILDREN OPEN-ENDED QUESTIONS

can't answer with a "Yes" or "No". Instead of 'Did you have a good day at school?' ask 'What was your day at school like?' Change 'Do you have homework?' to 'What do you have to do tonight for class tomorrow?' Try and word them so they can't get away with a single-word answer. If you didn't get the question right and they answer that way, ask again with it rephrased. Don't give up. Go to the mattresses!

Each child is different so the length of time and persistence that is required will vary. Jared seemed to be born talking. He never had a problem expressing himself. Bonnie had him with her one time when she was shopping. He was two. He kept grabbing things from the shelves as they passed by. She told him to stop it. The next time he grabbed something she took it from him and gave him a light smack on the hand. He was indignant. 'That hurt! You hurt me. My hand hurts now! Why did you hurt me?' She wanted to gag him to get him out of the store. When we asked him what he did at school we got the whole nine yards. Being five years younger than the oldest two he was well steeped in the tradition. He would give you every minute detail. With him we had to encourage the ability to be a little more succinct. So we went back to more 'closed' questions. 'Did you enjoy that? Did you have maths today?'

We also worked on their sense of humour. We would tell them 'knock, knock' jokes and laugh hilariously with them. We would persevere through the jokes they told with no punch line and laugh heartily with them. They inherited the ability to mix up the punch line from their Dad. They outgrew it, he didn't. We would quote funny lines from films. We would do silly things at times to get laughs. They would bring joke books home from the library and read us every one.

As they got older they became more witty and humorous. It seems to be about the age of twelve where you will find yourself the brunt of their humour. This is good because you need to laugh at yourself. By doing so you teach them to lighten up and not take themselves so seriously. While they are honing this skill there is a line where on one side the jibe at you is funny but on the other side they have disrespected you. They need to be taught when they have crossed the line. You have to tell them as simply as 'you crossed the line.

That was disrespectful.' Make sure your face lines up with your comment or the effectiveness of it will be lost. You can't tell them they crossed a line if you have a big grin on your face. Ask them to apologise and then forgive them. We had to do it with all the children. Trial and error is how we all learn.

When I was thirteen I took art lessons on a Saturday morning with 12 really cute girls. I was a fairly good artist and really enjoyed art in school. I was much better than my friends. If I was good, why did I take lessons? There were many techniques and skills that I didn't know that would make my work easier and better. I had a natural talent for it but I needed training in the tricks of the trade. Needless to say being a hormonally challenged young male in a class of young women I learned nothing about art. But boy, did I enjoy the classes! Never missed one! Conversation is an art. The natural talent and inclination may be there but with the help of some old masters a child can become really proficient.

POINTS TO PONDER

1. Do you listen to your children when they are speaking?

2. How can you encourage your child to communicate?

3. Is your child inquisitive?

4. What type of question would inspire your child to speak more?

Team Sport 16

Parenting is ideally a team sport. During a game we have all said or witnessed another fan yell out 'What are you doing? Pass the ball! Oh for goodness sake this is a team sport, pass to the other players!' The post game interviews always have the star of the game humbly stating that the team played well and that he/she couldn't have scored without them. It is not simply rhetorical, it is the truth. The player who stole the ball from the opposing team and then passed it on is as much responsible for the goal as the striker is who put it in the net. One person cannot take on 11 and win. No matter how good they are they need the support of the whole team.

Parenting is a team activity requiring full participation from all the members. We have often wondered how single parents have survived, other than the fact that they have no option. As a single parent you at least don't face contradiction by the other parent. Often because of a lack of agreement the children can run riot because one doesn't back up the other. One parent thinks that something is not important but the other does. One tries to correct behaviour that the other condones.

Kids are not stupid. They instinctively know how to play one parent off against the other. If they want something or are doing something they shouldn't, they know they will get away with it if Mummy and Daddy aren't in agreement. If I can bounce on the furniture when Mummy's away, then I will do it when she is home. I will keep trying to do it until Daddy says "Stop".

A lack of agreement will undermine the training you are doing with your child. You do have to realise as parents that you are training your child to be a responsible adult. You are instilling in them your values and the cultural values of your country. You are the teacher responsible for their education. What you do at home determines what teachers can do at school. Their role is to enhance what you are doing in your home. To leave the responsibility for discipline to them is to

CHILD REARING REQUIRES AGREEMENT BY ALL PARENTS INVOLVED

110

abdicate your responsibility. A teacher is only with your child for ten months of one year. You are with them until they leave home and you continue to be in some depth of relationship with them the rest of your life. Parenting is more than coexisting with this person you and your spouse created. It is active, intelligent interaction with your child.

If you do not talk about what you both consider to be reasonable or important, you will contradict each other. You also dishonour one another before your children. If I say something is important and you disregard it, you have dishonoured me. By doing this in front of the children you are teaching them to dishonour your spouse. The interesting thing about that is they not only learn to dishonour your spouse but they come to dishonour you. This is what you have taught them about family life. I believe it is the reason that teens can become so disconnected from their parents. They see the lack of respect their parents demonstrate towards each other and intuitively feel a lack of trust for them. You can't dishonour someone in front of another and not unsettle your child. They will think "If you did it to them you will do it to me".

Your relationship is also teaching them about marriage. Schools do not offer a marriage course along with maths and literature. Somehow we are just supposed to know what it takes to be a good partner. The only example your children have is you. They will do what you did. If you were devious in your dealings, they will be as well. If you are forthright, they will be too. If you are truthful, they will be. If you lie to your spouse, they will too. If you respect them, they will as well. If you dishonour them, they will too. Your children may not want to follow through on the negative habits but they will still tend to replicate your patterns. Only very thoughtful and analytical people seem to be able to break the trend.

If you agree, then support each other's decisions in front of the children. If you don't agree, talk it through when the two of you are alone. Often we think we are on the same page when we aren't. We just assume the other one is in agreement. We usually do things the way our family did it. Our spouse usually does things the way their family did. This works fine as long as the families did things the same way. My wife assumed I would do what her father did. If something broke, he tried to fix it. If he made it worse, he got it repaired. My father immediately called in a repairman if something broke. His attitude was: leave it to the expert. When we first got married, Bonnie would tell me something broke. I would say, "Call a repairman". Even though she heard me she heard it through her filter of "Dad always fixes things". She wouldn't call anyone. I would ask several days later if it was fixed. She would say, "Oh, you fixed it". My response was, "No, I thought you were calling someone to do it". We had to discuss our expectations and correct them, as we were now a new family.

If you don't agree, don't correct each other in front of the children. If it needs an immediate response, draw aside, discuss it and come to a mutual agreement. Then announce it to the kids. Say something like 'Your father and I have just discussed the issue and we have agreed to (whatever).' This way you are presenting a united front and teaching them how to manage decision- making as a couple. If you continue to disrespect one another by not working on agreement, you will undermine your relationship. You will make judgements about one another, which can cause you to start to dislike the other person. A lack of respect will eventually create a like reaction in your spouse. Love is built on respect for one another. You wouldn't have been attracted to the other person in the first place if you didn't feel an initial level of respect and admiration for them. Expressions of respect and honour will continue to build a strong marriage and strong children.

POINTS TO PONDER

As a single parent you will find these questions helpful if the other parent is involved through joint custody. If they are involved in parenting, you need to work on supporting one another in relationship to the children.

1. Do you have agreement regarding your child's behaviour?

2. Have you discussed with your spouse/partner what you desire to see in your child ?

3. Are there times when you feel dishonoured? Why?

4. Do any of your spouse/partner's actions make you feel like not supporting them?

What? Me, Angry!

Discipline is a very misused word. In common usage it would probably be understood to mean 'punishing your child for wrongdoing'. When people ask for advice on discipline, they are usually asking for the appropriate punishment for disobedience. 'What would you do in this situation? Would you spank them or put them in their room?' They are looking for something to effect a change. There is no punishment that works like a magic wand. If you say 'No' to your child erratically, their behaviour won't improve. If you have them go to a quiet spot, they won't magically change if you don't follow through time after time. As has been stated before within the book, it is the consistency of your correction that makes a difference. It is the self-sacrifice to leave what you are really enjoying to bring correction. When we knew we were having number three, we realised that it was just more dying for us. You have to die to your own comforts and your own desires for a number of years. In fact you may have to lay some things down permanently. Like eating all the crispy ginger beef yourself. Believe me if you like it they will too!

Consistency can never be stressed enough. Children need to know that when you draw a line, if they cross it, you will do something. You are setting boundaries that actually make them feel secure. They feel the assurance of your love for them. Some times they are acting up to get your attention. They want to know if you still love them. We were recently at a resort and a boy of about 8 or 9 called his mother from the pool. She ignored him. He called again and again every time coming closer. Finally he was standing next to her calling her before she glared at him and told him to be quiet. Later she went to get the inflatable mattress, which he grabbed before her. He floated out on the pool, wanting her to respond. She turned away, went back to her sun bed and ignored him. She was frustrated but so was he. He wanted some attention: good, bad or ugly. This mother was acting consistently, only she was reinforcing what to her was his negative behaviour.

When you look at behaviour you don't like, deal with it. Don't wait until you are fuming mad and roaring with anger. That is when you will make some totally rash statement that you will regret. You may even strike in anger, which is inappropriate. You are larger and stronger and when in a rage empowered by adrenaline. You can do far more damage than you realise, both physically and emotionally. Remember to act in cold blood. Don't let situations gravitate to your boiling point. Respond calmly and your child will be less likely to be hysterical too.

When you punish your child, think about the consequences of what you are doing. Are you punishing yourself as well as them? This can often happen. You've said something, now you have to follow through. Once Bonnie had three of the kids at the grocery store. She had been having problems with them running around and grabbing things she didn't want them to touch. She told them if they continued, she would take them home immediately. They didn't believe her and kept horsing around. She felt really caught in a dilemma in that she had 98% of a major shop in her trolley and was so close to checking out. But if she wanted them to respect her word, she had to follow through. She left her cart and took the kids home. I was home when they arrived. Much to my surprise they went silently to their rooms. Until I saw her face! I wanted to go to my room too and I hadn't done anything. I spent the next half hour listening, comforting and encouraging her that she had done the right thing. It was effective, as she never had to do that again. The consequences though cost her in time and effort.

Children have a very different perception of time to ours. For us a day is 24 hours, for them it is as a 1000 years. The second day in a newborn's life is double their lifetime. A day to someone in their thirties is only a fraction of their existence. When you say "No television for a week", you might as well have assigned children to life in prison. A week is an incredibly long time especially under twelve. That's 7 sleeps. The problem with the week is you are also punishing yourself. You can't watch any TV while they are awake either. You also probably have to come up with some more activities to occupy them now, where you used to get half an hour to yourself while Bob the

> IF CORRECTION IS APPROPRIATE AND APPLIED CONSISTENTLY, IT WILL CREATE CHANGE

Builder was on. One day is usually sufficient to create a change in behaviour.

The other thing is 'get over it'. Correcting the behaviour with something that is quick and effective deals with the situation and lets all of you get on with life. Something that takes several days or a week doesn't let you get over it. Because young children are basically living for the moment, you then have to frequently recount to them the whole incident so that the correction makes sense. But unconsciously this teaches them to hold long accounts. It becomes more about payback then behaviour change. So they start to hold long accounts and resist forgiving quickly.

If the correction is appropriate, applied consistently, it will create change in actions. If it is inappropriate, as in too long, it will either create resentment, which reinforces other feelings, or it won't be followed through. Not following through will nullify the change you were trying to create in the first place.

Remember you are trying to deal with errant behaviour not run a penal colony. The choices you make potentially have just as big an effect on you as on them. If we are looking for consistency, then choose wisely so that you will continue to be consistent yourself.

POINTS TO PONDER

1. Do you have good follow through on your verbal commands?

2. Are your actions consistent with your words?

3. Is the correction generally appropriate for the level of your child's misbehaviour?

4. Do you regularly re-evaluate the consequences you have determined for correction? Are they still the best?

For Goodness Sake Lighten Up

Recently my sister-in-law and my brother visited London for the first time. I have taken many people around the city and they seem to enjoy it. They feel if they have seen Trafalgar Square, Big Ben and Westminster Abbey that they have basically 'done London'. My sister-in-law absorbed London. She breathed it, tasted it, and loved every minute of it. She would be on one side of the street, look across, give a huge exclamation and then run across the street to whatever caught her attention. She scoured Kensington Palace as if it might not be there tomorrow. She was in utter shock that in the six years I had lived in the country I had not visited it. She devoured it.

Some people go through life like most tourists visiting London. Been there, done that, bought the t- shirt. I imagine they are excited but their faces don't show it. My sister-in-law was excited, didn't care who knew it and thoroughly experienced London. That is the way life is supposed to be lived. Don't take for granted that there is another tomorrow for you. Enjoy the sunsets, even the sunrises, if you are unfortunate enough to see them, and live. Your children will reflect your same passion for life.

> LAUGH AND PLAY WITH YOUR CHILDREN

One of the most important parts of living is having fun. Did you know that laughing is good for you? Research is proving that laughing increases your body's capacity to heal.

We started having fun with the kids even as newborns. We would blow on their tummy, kiss their feet and tickle anywhere we could to get a reaction. We used to have crawling races with the twins. We would set them both up side by side on the kitchen floor, open the cupboard with the cereal boxes and they would take off. We would laugh and laugh over that. They loved it.

On every child's first birthday we would make them a chocolate cake loaded with icing and one candle. We dressed them only in a nappy and let them loose with the cake. The twins had cake where I thought it was impossible to get cake. Jared on the other hand was disgusted; he didn't like getting his hands messy. So we gave him a fork.

Bonnie and the kids used to chair dance on the way to school. They would put the music on really loud and then go crazy at every traffic light. They laughed even more at the other drivers' reactions. They still talk about chair-dancing.

Every one of the kids has ended up in the shower fully dressed at some time or another. The little monkeys would do something that would provoke a chase around the house and if they ended up in the bathroom, they were in trouble. I remember coming home to find the kids in the paddling pool. It was hot so I climbed in, clothes and all. Then we tried to soak Mummy. We used to have water fights with water guns, buckets and eventually hoses. When we washed the car, it was a great opportunity to get wet. The only goal of fishing was to wait long enough until one of them fell in.

When he was two, Jared would ride with me on a bike seat as I rode around the neighbourhood. He would sing at the top of his lungs whatever was his favourite tune at the moment. He would also come out when he was three and ride on the forklift with me after we had moved to the farm.

We played cards and games with them. To help Jess compete, we would partner with her. She used to love to play but hated the stress of trying to win. One time in a crucial tiebreaker she couldn't sit at the table with me and help. She paced back and forth and finally lamented 'tie breakers really piss me off'. She was only five and after the initial shock we laughed and chuckled about that for hours.

Play with them. Recreation is essential for a balanced life. We have had a few friends over the years that never knew how to have fun. Growing up they learned to work and to work hard. They started jobs early and worked constantly. They had no concept of fun. They would ask their wives if they were having fun yet. An interesting phenomenon is their children all started working early in life too. It wasn't only the Saturday part-time job. It was before school and after school. They didn't get into sports either. Life is more than work. There is a balance that is required for a quality lifestyle.

We have always played with the children. I have played sports with them in the garden from the time they could walk. We have a picture of Jessie at 2 with a ball glove playing back catcher for our home baseball game. I used to have boxing matches with them in the hallway of our house. I would let the boys wrestle me to the ground and gloat like champions. I pinned both of them when they each turned 5 to show them that I could if I wanted to. It was like a replay five years apart as both of them stood with their hands on their hips and said in utter disbelief 'I can't believe he did that! I always beat him before.'

We would plan trips to see new places to give them an increased experience and knowledge base. We didn't want them leaving home having never had the experience of anything other than home and school. We had a young lady come with us on one trip as a nanny to help with the children. She was 15 and had never seen an escalator.

Camping was an essential outing every summer. Campfires used to be such a hoot. The ritual was to start the fire in the morning and keep it stoked all day. After dinner we would roast marshmallows, burned black was my favourite. We would sing and act around the campfire in the evenings. We have had the park supervisors tell us to settle down as neighbouring campers had complained we were too loud and it was past 11 p.m.

Childrearing is not just about training children to be well behaved. It is about training children to be well-adjusted and well-rounded individuals. If all you ever concentrate on is their behaviour, they will grow to resent you. The ideal is to nurture children who know the way to go when they are on their own but that also want to have a relationship with you. To have that you need to play and have fun.

POINTS TO PONDER

1. What do you do to have fun?

2. Do you laugh with your kids?

3. What activities do you have planned as a family that are fun?

4. Take a moment to evaluate your family life. Is there a balance in your quality of lifestyle? What would you change if it isn't in balance?

Words

It's never only words. Words from a parent or an authority figure have a huge impact on children. They shape the future for little ones. When you tell them they will amount to nothing, it wounds them deeply. When you speak acceptance and love, they feel secure. Your words are powerful. Thoughtful choice of words can have a huge influence on your children.

Parents are leaders. A leader is one who has influence, evidenced by whether anyone is following. As a parent you are the one. Daddy and Mummy are the names of the two most significant leaders in their life. Your children will follow you. They will imitate you and your actions.

One day I was driving with Bonnie and our youngest child who was still in her car seat. Just as the traffic light changed to green,

Jess shouted out, 'Come on lady, move.' We were both surprised and I asked Bonnie where she got that from. A few days later I heard myself shouting out, 'Come on lady, move.'

A very disciplined friend of ours told us a story about his son when he was five. Gene would follow the same routine every day of the week before leaving for work. At the end of getting ready for the day he would sit in his favourite recliner with a book and ponder for fifteen minutes or so. One Saturday morning he and his wife found their son sitting on Daddy's recliner attired with white shirt, tie and dress trousers reading a book. He even had applied aftershave for the full effect.

A co-worker of German descent told me that they have a proverb in their language that means essentially the apple doesn't fall too far from the tree. This is so true. Your children are shaping themselves in the image of one of you. They will reflect your good and your bad qualities, although the bad always seems to be magnified a hundred times. When our oldest two were in their teens, we led a youth group, which met in our home. After the evening was over and the parents were picking up their teenagers, our daughter would run outside in her stocking feet to hug her friends good-bye. Bonnie would get so upset and snort, 'what did she think she is doing?' I would graciously remind her that it was exactly what she did when our friends were leaving. The thing that bugged Bonnie was the very thing she, herself, did all the time. Our daughter was only imitating what she had seen her mother doing for years.

I once counselled a young woman who told me that she had not been sexually active until she came home later than her mother's curfew. Her mother was in a rage and accused her daughter of being a little whore. Her words wounded so deeply that this young lady told me that she thought if this is what her mother thought of her than it must be true. From that time on she acted out what she had been accused of. Her mother spoke a self- fulfilling judgement over her daughter. Ten years later she was getting help in an attempt to sort out her devastated life.

WORDS ARE POWERFUL AND CAN DEEPLY AFFECT YOUR CHILD

As I grew up, my father had a habit of pointing out what I couldn't do. He would tell me I could never play goalie in hockey, as my eyes weren't good enough. He would tell me that my eyes were crossing to the point where I became so self-conscious I could not look at anyone face on in case my eyes crossed. I was always too slow or too fat or too young to do things.

When I was in school, I was quite good academically. I would bring my report card home with marks in the high 90s. He would inevitably ask me where the other marks were. I do not remember him saying "Well done" or "That was excellent". In the fifth grade I was in a tooth and nail fight for highest average in the class. I remember having an 89.3 average, my friend had 89.5 and our girl friend had 89.7. I was mortified that I would have to go home and hear how Dad stood at the top of his class all the time. 0.4 of a mark was causing me depression. Why? The most important person in my life never spoke a positive encouraging word to me. As most little boys I desperately wanted to be like my Dad, to be acceptable in his sight, to hear him say "Well done".

I finally gave up. I knew I couldn't please him so I just worked at a pace to keep up with my peer group. If they were excelling, then I would work to excel. If they thought a mid 60 mark was an attempt to make them look bad, I lowered my efforts to conform and survive. My father had an opportunity to build self-confidence and self esteem into me with a few simple words. He didn't and I suffered for it. We all did actually because my poor work ethic became a source of concern for them in my high school years. My mother used to say to me that I was cutting off my nose to spite my face. I never understood until much later.

When I met my future wife, she spoke positive affirming words to me. I was embarrassed because I didn't know what do with such kind words. I didn't know how to react. No one had told me that I was handsome or smart before. I loved it but struggled with believing that she could actually mean it. With time I started to enjoy the approbation. Now I am a big suck for it. If I give a speech, afterwards I'll unabashedly beg for it. "I need, I need..." Was I good? I knew it, thank you. Thank you.

Bonnie had grown up in a home with very affirming parents. She simply imitated her mother when she told me how wonderful I was. She had witnessed her own mother saying the same things to her father. It became natural. When we had children, it was natural for her to tell them how wonderful they were, how well they were doing and how beautiful and handsome they were. It wasn't that way for me. I struggled to be positive. I had learned to accentuate the negative, ignore the positive. But having benefited myself from her positive encouragement I knew that it was something I should imitate. Often we meet people who say 'we never did that in our family' as if it is cast in stone and cannot now be changed. So, even though it was a demoralising, devastating habit in your family, you will continue to do it to your own children. We have a choice to do things differently. You can learn new methods if you try. I have. I don't feel as natural at it as my wife seems to be but I still do it.

All people respond to kind and loving words. They will work harder and change behaviour in response to kind words. Your children don't always have to be corrected by pointing out the negative. You can shape their attitudes and behaviour by emphasising the positive. They will grow into your affirmations. You may never have experienced it yourself but you have the power within yourself to give it to someone else and change the way they see themselves.

POINTS TO PONDER

1. Were your parents affirming or derogatory towards you?

2. What would you like to have had said to you?

3. What are some of the positive attributes of your child?

4. Try speaking positively about these attributes and observe how your child responds. Does it have a positive effect on them?

Not 20 Their Friend

Children are wonderful. They can be a great source of love and fulfilment. When I first started school teaching, I was getting love and affirmation from my class. They didn't know that I hadn't been athletic or the president of the class or the king of the prom. They were in awe of their teacher. Parents would come into the interviews on Meet the Teacher nights and say all that they had heard at home was "Mr. Inkster says" and "Mr. Inkster thinks". I was like a god.

Then we had our own children and I didn't need my class to tell me how wonderful I was. I had my sons and daughters who would light up and squeal with delight when I came home from work. I couldn't do anything wrong in their eyes. They wanted to be with me, to go where I went and they liked what I liked. They met a deep need in me. That need has to be met by a power greater than a human but I didn't know that initially.

If I hadn't had that need met by the right source, I would probably have continued seeking affirmation and acceptance from my children. This presents a significant problem when the time comes for you to make decisions for their benefit that they may not like. If you are worried about being their friend or about falling off the pedestal, then you won't make the right decision. You'll abdicate for fear they won't like you.

Recently one of my granddaughters has thought I am the next best thing to sliced bread. Grandpa can do no wrong. It was a very heady place to be. On one occasion she hurt herself and came to me instead of her mother. Wow! Then I had the opportunity to wrap her up in a big towel after her bath and to take her to the lounge. She started to squirm and cry loudly to get out of the towel. I made the mistake of telling her to ask nicely and I would let her go. She wouldn't. I was in a predicament. If I let her go, it would reinforce that type of behaviour. But if I didn't let her go, I risked losing my valued status. I chose to hold her until she stopped shouting. When she stopped, I let her go and told her how good it was to ask nicely. It was a tough choice. I was not very popular after that. But the issue which parents face, even more than grandparents is, do you do what is right for your child or do you try to be their friend and keep their admiration?

If you try to be their friend instead of a caring, responsible parent, the very thing you feared will come upon you. Your children will resent you for not fulfilling the role of a parent. They will be upset because you didn't give them what they needed when they needed it. Friends they have, its parents they need. Remember parents are leaders and leaders make the hard decisions that friends aren't able to.

You will sometimes find yourself in a love-hate relationship with your children. They will tell you they hate you when they don't get their own way. It will make you feel awful but it is only a manipulative ploy to get their way. They will be upset with you because you tell them to go to bed when they need it. Their friends may all stay up later but the issue for you to decide is whether keeping up with the crowd is the right thing for your child. You know your child better than anyone else so make your decisions based on that knowledge.

When children move into the teen years they need you more than ever to be a parent for them. The peer pressure is phenomenal and overwhelming. To say no to friends is to lose face, and more than likely to lose friends, and to put them in a place of isolation. We had an agreement with our children that if they were faced with a situation where they didn't want to participate but would lose face if they refused they could say, "My parents say no". They could then join in with all the big bad parent conversations and still be part of their community. They would answer the phone; say "I'll ask my parents", then mouth to us, "I don't want to go". At that point we would say in a loud clear voice that they definitely couldn't go. Then they would tell their friends how we wouldn't let them go. After the conversation they would thank us. We knew that their friends sometimes thought of us as the big, old sticks in the mud but we didn't care. We weren't there for their pleasure. We were there for the welfare of our children.

> THE RIGHT CHOICE FOR YOUR CHILD WILL NOT ALWAYS MAKE YOU POPULAR

When they are young, children need someone who will protect them, set boundaries, teach them, guide and encourage them. It is essential when they are very young. As they mature, you will find your role gradually changing. They will be making their own decisions and will have to establish their own boundaries. All the things you so diligently taught them will eventually be internalised. They will have established values, confidence, and an ability to think through issues that concern them. Hopefully they will be secure in your love and able to look to you for assistance when they need it.

You are their advocate as well. There will be times when our young people need someone to stand on their behalf and confront those who are taking advantage of their youthfulness. You may have to confront a teacher or employer for them. We have taught our children to respect authority figures and to be obedient when under their care and direction. We are not in favour of attacking educators when your children are not doing well but to work with them for the greater good of the child.

Having said that, there are times when they need you to plead their case. Our two oldest children had a paper route when they were twelve. We wanted them to learn responsibility and a work ethic as well as some money. So every morning one of us got up at 6:30 am with them and drove them around their paper route so that it was done before 7 am. We did this because the route was very long. In the winter the mornings were dark. We didn't want anything to happen to them. One Saturday afternoon their supervisor came around to speak with them. I was in the office and hadn't been party to the start of the conversation. As I came down the hall I could see something was wrong by the looks on their faces. I asked him what the situation was. He had been berating them for not delivering the papers on time as he had had a complaint. I could see they didn't have the nerve to tell him otherwise so they stood there taking his comments and getting more and more discouraged. I intervened. I told him that his complaint was wrong. That Bonnie or I drove them every morning so that the papers would be there before 7 am. I told him that instead of believing the worst about his employees who had not had any previous complaints, he should have checked with us first. I told him that he risked losing two reliable employees because he hadn't done his homework first. As I did so I must have kept walking towards him for our conversation, which started in the hall of the house, ended with him standing by his car on the street and me standing in the driveway. In this situation I saw my children as being unjustly accused and unable to defend themselves. It was my role to defend them. A parent has the authority and right to do this for them. A friend doesn't.

With maturity they will come to view you not only as their beloved parent but also as a good friend. Then you can have a rich friendship created from a sacrificial relationship.

POINTS TO PONDER

1. Do you ever think that your child will hate you because you are firm?

2. Are you looking to your child for affirmation? Are you looking for them to be a friend to you?

3. Who is leading in your home?

4. Is your child facing peer pressure? How can you help?

Does your child need you to be an advocate in some area of their life?

Don't Punish Yourself

When I was training to be a teacher, one of the key points made by the faculty advisor was not to punish yourself while disciplining your class. The same thing applies to parents. If you are not careful, you may end up punishing yourself while attempting to correct your children's behaviour.

If you are really upset and tell them they can't watch television for a week, you are punishing yourself. Television can be an effective educational tool, which teaches your child concepts and provides a quiet time for you. No TV includes all shows and that particular show you like as well. If your home isn't particularly large, you may have no option as to whether you watch TV or not. Until they go to bed you're banned as well.

This is why we advocate correction in cold blood. If you are upset, you won't think logically or calmly about the consequences of your actions. If you correct a behaviour that is unacceptable before it gets out of hand, you are far more likely to choose a truly effective punishment. If you correct an action early before things have escalated, a lighter penalty may suffice. It may be enough to talk to them eye to eye or have them sit on a chair to settle down. Keeping in mind that we are at work all the time with little ones, we will be more alert to dealing with issues quicker. If we allow things to go unchecked, the consequences are less pleasant for everyone.

What you are trying to do is to create a win-win situation for yourself and your child. You want to correct behaviour effectively without causing yourself a great deal of anxiety. Some people suffer from physical distress when faced with any form of confrontation, so subsequently leave misbehaviour unchecked too long. The result of ignoring it actually causes them to feel the effects of increased adrenalin and the displeasure of being angry. The key is to respond early.

Remember talking at your children is not always sufficient. As we have said before you have to walk the talk for it to be effective. When children are small, they have limited vocabularies so they need to have actions validating words. If you tell them to stop and they don't, go and get them. You don't have to be mad when you do it. Just do it! If you have told them to come here and they don't, go and get them repeating the words. "I said come here and this is here."

It isn't uncommon to see parents who are not very happy with their children. They are embarrassed by the lack of response when they are in public. They feel trapped in a no-win situation. Their children aren't responding and everyone around them is aware and judging them for that. They need to do something but their children are making it extremely difficult to save face with their peers. Unfortunately children's public display of inappropriate behaviour is indicative of a lack of respect at home too.

The only one who can do something about it is you, the parent. You deserve what you tolerate. If you tolerate back talk at home, you will get it in public. If you tolerate misbehaviour at home you will get more in public. In fact what you tolerate is like seed. It reproduces after its own kind but it multiplies.

YOU DESERVE WHAT YOU TOLERATE

In essence, if you don't correct inappropriate behaviour, you are punishing yourself. The embarrassment in public when your children are acting up is very hard to swallow. The fact that you can't enjoy being some where because your children are a problem, punishes you. When you feel harassed at home because it seems that you don't have a moment's peace, your lack of discipline is punishing you.

Discipline or training for your child reflects on your personal discipline. If you are consistent, you will reap the rewards of well-behaved children. If you are inconsistent, you will reap the hassle of poorly behaved children. The consequences of tolerance are the sense of having condemned yourself to a life of constant tension. You have punished yourself by not appropriately guiding your child.

It is easy to shrug off certain behaviour when children are young because it seems inconsequential. The problem with ignoring annoying actions is they are likely to occur again and again each time becoming more entrenched in their life. They can become habitual and usually more prominent with time. When Joel was two he spat for some reason that was actually quite cute. We chuckled which caused him to do it again. He thought he was funny and wanted to make us laugh. Although at two it was funny and not very significant in volume, we decided we needed to stop him because we didn't think it would be cute at 8 or 10 or older. You may think that is severe or over the top but we didn't. We thought that it was funny this time but it won't be later. So we told him to stop. It is easy to stop when something isn't a habit. Breaking habits are far more difficult. Ask anyone who has tried to break one.

To not take action is to punish yourself. Eventually it will come back to haunt you. T o correct in anger or frustration will inevitably result in punishment that you will regret. The reason most people have children is the thought that they will bring great joy into their life. They will if you are wise not to punish yourself.

POINTS TO PONDER

1. Are you pleased with the way your children behave in public?

2. Are you tolerating something in your child that needs to change?

3. What consequences would be good for your child and still acceptable for you?

4. Think through a scenario in your mind so that when the situation occurs you can respond in a calm and confident manner.

Security in Boundaries **22**

In the mid 90s we bought a house that was huge. It was so big that initially we didn't know what to do with all the space. The kitchen had room for a sizeable island in the middle of it that didn't create any shortage of floor space. It also had a family room next to the dining area in the kitchen. Then it had a lounge and formal dining room, another family room, 4 bathrooms and 6 bedrooms. The first two to three months we all lived in the kitchen and family room. We didn't know what to do with all the extra space. We felt insecure because our boundaries had suddenly been expanded way beyond anything we had known before. Eventually we became accustomed to all the space and newfound freedom. Once again we felt secure within our new boundaries.

Boundaries are an essential part of life.

Social occasions often cause a great deal of distress to adults when they are new. The reason is they aren't sure of the boundaries. What is expected? How will I be received? What is the dress code? Will I have acceptable manners? Will I know anyone? All these questions go through our minds before we actually attend, if we even do. Some adults will chicken out rather than deal with all the uncertainty.

One of my friends recently told me how helpful a particular personality test had been for him. He found that in his specific group everyone felt the same amount of stress that he did about entering a room full of people. He told me that he would either wait outside a social event until he had planned his entrance strategy or alternatively enter the room seeking privacy for five minutes or more so that he could suss out the lay of the land. He found social gatherings very exhausting. This really surprised me, as he seemed to handle them so well and was very gregarious.

My point, if it has escaped you, is adults need to know their boundaries to feel secure. If fully-grown mature adults feel insecure, how much more does a child need security? If parents don't provide adequate boundaries, a child will feel very insecure. How they respond will depend on the personality of each child but they will definitely react to the lack of security. Some will withdraw, others will go wild. Both responses are the result of not knowing the boundaries.

A lack of security will leave a child feeling unloved. If they don't feel protected and secure, they will think you don't love them enough to protect them. In their minds they somehow know that the role of a parent is to create an environment where they feel secure. If you don't clearly display boundaries for them, they may push and push in an attempt to define their boundaries. The mistake that is often made by parents is to assume that the pushing and pushing is the child's attempt to exert their independence. The reality is they are looking for the edge.

Once they have found the edge they may push against it to see if it holds. They are simply looking for the reassurance that you still love them and are concerned for them. They are happy that there is an edge. They may act like it is

> BOUNDARIES CREATE SECURITY, PROTECTION AND LOVE

upsetting but ultimately it is creating a feeling of security within them. The other problem with boundaries is to not allow them to enlarge with the child who is growing older. How you protected them at five is not going to fit with them at ten or thirteen. I used to watch a family

I know who did this with their children. One of the most embarrassing things for their oldest child was the father correcting him in front of others when the young man was in his mid to late teens. This kind of correction is appropriate when children are much younger and are not as socially aware of their surroundings. At a younger age you often have to correct them on the spot, as they are not aware of what is appropriate behaviour in the situation. For example, you are at a party and are engaged in conversation, when your seven year old interrupts by pulling on your coat and talking right over the conversation. At that point it is appropriate to stop them, point out that you are in the middle of a conversation and that it is impolite to interrupt. You may then tell them to wait until you are finished before you will talk with them. When they are in their teens, they should be socially aware of their surroundings and how to behave. To correct them in this situation is hurtful as they are now well tuned into the social dynamics.

Boundaries have to grow with your child. We found our new home daunting because of its size but soon grew into the larger place. Children need to have their boundaries increased just as much as they have to have their clothes replaced because they have outgrown them. When our children reached their teens, we stopped telling them what time to go to bed. We didn't let them know we were doing it. It was funny to watch each one of them stay up later and later. They thought they were getting away with something and were enjoying the feeling that somehow we had overlooked them. Finally as each one experienced their first night of liberty they would come to us and ask us why we hadn't told them to go to bed yet. At that point we would inform them that they were old enough now to choose their own bedtime. They then dragged themselves off to bed. The first night was the only night that they stayed up to a completely irresponsible time. The next night they were so tired they went to bed early and of their own choosing.

At one point our oldest daughter asked us if we would help her set some boundaries. She said she just could not say no to her friends when they asked her to do things. She was overwhelmed with activities and favours she was fulfilling for people. We agreed to help her and would talk over each request as they came in. We were teaching her how to set priorities for her time and to reassure her that her friends would still love her if she said no to them. Don't assume that setting boundaries is intuitive for everyone. Each personality style has different strengths and weaknesses. Some just know what to do in certain situations, yet are helpless in others. In this case Becky's personality is very outgoing and friendly which has opened many relationships to her. She also has a very serving nature. These are wonderful traits but can leave her feeling taken advantage of. No one person was dominating her, it was simply the volume of requests from everyone in total that was exhausting her.

Boundaries are essential for wholeness in a person's development. Experts on dysfunction say the problem with many of the people trapped in this is incompleteness in forming boundaries that defined their being. Boundaries, leading to soundness of character, are developed in a child by being put in place by their parents. Don't be afraid to put them in place. Equally, don't be rigid in not allowing them to change. Life is full of change and nothing stays the same. Certainly your family dynamics won't stay the same because you have children who are growing and maturing. If you are uncomfortable with change, you will have to work harder at being more flexible. Think ahead so you are prepared for change. Most times discomfort with change is simply caused by it being sprung on you without warning.

POINTS TO PONDER

1. Do you have boundaries set for your children?

2. Are you consistent with the boundaries?

3. Describe a time when your child has pushed the boundary.

4. Did they get the secure love they were looking for?

Children Are Hard Work

A few years ago a young couple we knew well had a beautiful baby boy. They were over at our house one evening after the birth and we asked all the questions one does about the whole delivery. The mother said the most amazing thing about the delivery was how much hard work it was. In my usual sensitive thoughtful way I said, "Why do you think they call it labour?" She said it had never occurred to her that this was involved. Fortunately the human race doesn't connect this word with its meaning when it comes to having babies. The delivery is only the beginning of the labour involved in raising children.

Some would say childrearing is a labour of love, which is true, although it is challenging to keep a loving perspective when you have been up all night with a teething baby. Children are full-time employment. There are

157

many benefits but seldom vacations with pay. In fact you take them with you when you are trying to take a break from your other career.

We know that many young fathers find the newborn stage the hardest to cope with. The reason usually is that the baby isn't physically able to do anything, like wrestle or ride a bike or kick a ball. But it is such an essential stage for young parents' conditioning. It is the initial stage of your marathon training. You begin with the loss of sleep. Remember when you could sleep through the night and lie in on Saturdays and Sundays? Now 7:30 am is a luxury. If you got the full force of the package right at the beginning, you would disintegrate.

When Bonnie and I were just married, we had the opportunity to take care of our two-year-old nephew for the weekend. We had him from Friday night through until Sunday. I have never been so exhausted by a Monday. I was glad to go to work and get a break. It always amazes us how one newborn or toddler can keep up to five adults fully occupied taking care of their needs. As grandparents we love it when the grandkids come but are exhausted by the time they leave. We are not conditioned for that kind of labour anymore.

The work never stops. The other day two of the grandchildren came to visit with their mother. Somewhere in the process of them getting ready to go home I was anointed with some recently consumed lunch. As they were pulling out of the drive my daughter-in-law inquired as to what the lovely orange stuff was on my shoulder. She then had the nerve to sit there laughing. One previously clean shirt to the laundry!

Laundry never stops. When our twins were in nappies, we used cloth ones. After we got them to bed in the evening I would go to the top floor of the house and pick up one of the nappy pails, which weighed about forty pounds with the disinfectant fluid besides the load of nappies. I would carry it down one flight where I picked up the second bucket of nappies. I would proceed down to the laundry room where I would take a load of nappies out of the dryer. Then I would take a load of nappies from the washing machine and transfer them into the dryer. Then I would pour out the disinfecting fluid in each bucket into the drain and then dump the nappies into the washing machine. With both machines on, I would take the load of dried ones upstairs to the lounge where Bonnie and I would sit folding them for the next fifteen minutes.

This was the time when we usually discovered that our dinner had burned in the oven. Probably it was the relief of smelling clean nappies instead of dirty that sharpened our senses enough to recognise the aroma of burning meat. Our children wonder why we like burned toast and popcorn. By the time we got to the food we were too tired to throw it out and start again. Once you have acquired the taste for charcoal there is nothing quite like it. Bonnie and I fight over the burned bits of popcorn. Our ungrateful children turn their noses up at burned popcorn as not good enough to eat. Why would anybody eat popcorn any other way is beyond me? It is so bland.

Training your children is hard work. Take temper tantrums for example. You can try and ignore them but they won't go away. They are the full-blown manifestation of the self-centred selfish will of a child. It's all about me. Our oldest daughter was classic in this case. When she was older, people would complement us on what a sweet spirit she had. They would add, if they had very self-willed children, the caveat that we wouldn't understand what it was like to have a strong-willed child. Believe me, all children are strong willed. It is what you do to mould their will that is important. Remember children are hard work and require stamina if you are to succeed in training them to be nice people whom others want to be around.

PARENTING IS HARD, LABOUR INTENSIVE WORK THAT IS BEST SUSTAINED BY LOVE

Becky had a terrible temper and strong

will from a small baby through to being a toddler. She would get so angry that her whole face would go red and her lower lip would stick out. Some times she cried and cried when nothing seemed wrong. She was fed, had slept, was dry, and was being loved. Yet she would cry and cry in anger. (You can tell the difference between a hurt cry and a mad cry). I would put her in her cot and tell her that when she had stopped I would pick her up. There was no point having her act this way in the lounge where her crying made it impossible for anyone to do anything else let alone be able to think.

I would wait outside her door until she stopped and then rush in and pick her up. If she started again, I would put her back down and tell her she needed to stop. I would again wait outside her door for her to go quiet and then rush back in. I would say to her, "That was great and I forgive you for being mad". Bonnie asked me if I was going to keep standing outside her door waiting for her to stop. I said I was. I didn't want to miss the moment when she stopped so that I could reinforce the good behaviour. It only took one session for her to get the idea that 'cot meant stop'. She soon got the message. Even though she got the message it didn't mean she stopped pulling these tantrums. But she learned that there were consequences to her unacceptable behaviour. When she got into a tantrum like this, Bonnie or I would pick her up, tell her she was going to bed until she stopped, and then take her to her room. As she got the idea that she wasn't going to win she quickly learned to stop crying and once she could talk say that she was sorry. I would forgive her and bring her back to the room where her brother was.

Now we know there are those who would say, "I don't agree with taking her to her cot as she will learn to hate it and not want to go to sleep in it anymore". I suppose this could happen if you left the child indefinitely without responding when they became quiet. But we didn't leave her. As soon as she quietened down we were in there, reinforcing the self-control she was exhibiting. After the first session, which seemed like an eternity but in reality lasted no more than a couple of minutes, she was never in her cot more than a few seconds. (Let me also assure you that she never had a problem sleeping.)

The change took place because we consistently followed through. It was a labour but it was well worth it. The nappy changing and washing was a labour but in the end was also well worth it. The visits for parent-teacher interviews were a labour but well worth it. We never missed one. I believe it said to our children that their education was important to us. As we look upon our children from this stage of life we see the labour was well worth it and truly was inspired by love.

POINTS TO PONDER

1. Do you find your children hard work?

2. Are there times that you resent all the work?

3. Is there anything you can implement that will help lighten the load?

4. Can you picture your child responding to you without having to get up or intervene?

Don't Assume

One of the most destructive elements I have witnessed over the years in relationships is assumption. What does assumption mean? It means that something is believed to be true without proof, like when we believe something that is not actually verified. Assumption is essentially taking for granted that you and the other person involved in a relationship are on the same page.

It is also emotionally charged, for with assumption comes the tendency to expect too much. We expect that the other person values what we value, thinks like we think, and will respond as we would respond. We may enter a relationship with absolute faith that everything will be fantastic and that we will live happily ever after. When the other person doesn't respond as we assumed they would, we are shocked. We are confused as to why they did

165

what they did. We feel disappointment because it is hurtful. "If they were for me," we assume, "then why would they do something that I would never consider doing?" Assumptions often lead to broken relationships.

When one person has unspoken assumptions, the other person is at an immediate disadvantage in the relationship. I have experienced such a relationship. We had a fellow join us in one of our endeavours. Over a three-year period we would have sessions where he would grill me on decisions and actions we had pursued. I constantly felt judged but couldn't figure out why. Finally we had a blow-up that resulted in the dissolution of our relationship. In the parting process he sent a letter in which he told me that he knew I didn't like him from the first day we met. He made an assumption that he felt was truth and then let it affect all of our interaction. No wonder I felt judged. He saw everything through the veil of rejection. It was inevitable that the relationship would collapse under those conditions.

DON'T ASSUME... DISCUSS YOUR INDIVIDUAL EXPECTATIONS

I have seen assumptions destroy marriages and business partnerships. When we entered into one financial relationship involving a house, our lawyer insisted that we have an escape clause. Both parties involved argued that it would be absolutely unnecessary. We felt that we were in this for life. The lawyer would not be moved from his position. We put the clause into the agreement to appease him, thinking that we would never invoke its use. Four years later we used the clause to dissolve the partnership amicably. The problem with assumptions is we are oblivious to them. We don't know we have them until we travel down the road together for a while. Because assumptions expect too much the effect is significant.

Two close friends entered into a business partnership without a contract. When I suggested that they draw up a contract, they reacted adamantly that they were like brothers and didn't need to do things that way. I told them it wasn't an implication about the quality of their relationship but a safeguard for them both to understand each other's expectations. They didn't heed the advice. The rest is history. One took the company into money losing ventures and the other resented it. Their relationship ended up ship wrecked with neither one talking to the other.

Assumption is often a huge source of marital stress in the area of child rearing. One parent has one assumption, the other has another. Neither one tells the other. They simply get madder and madder at their spouse. They think as that one fellow did with me, that everything the other person is doing is to sabotage them. They may even think that their mate is intent on making them into the big, bad parent so that they can win the children to themselves. They can think it is an issue of favouritism. The partner may not have a single thought that way.

It is very important that you meditate on what potential assumptions are playing out between you and your partner. Don't let the assumptions undermine and destroy your relationship. Start asking yourself the 'what if' questions. What if I am doing something from my childhood that she is unaware of? What if I am projecting my fear of my father onto my husband? What if I am trying to avoid something I hated my parents for doing but I haven't told my spouse?

Recently my son said to me how amazed he was that the hurts of the past so unconsciously affect our decisions of today. It is so true. We make a resolution over something that happened to us as a child and then make adult decisions based on it. The vow may be well buried in our subconscious but it has a profound effect upon how we think. We may avoid certain people, places or things because of it.

Spousal support is so essential for

raising children. You both need to be on the same page so that there is consistency in how you respond to your children. What you are trying to do, the values you are trying to instil, the behaviour you want to see are all determined by your consistency as a couple. If you constantly contradict each other, you will undermine all that you desire to see in your children.

Being a parent is one of the most taxing jobs in the world. We have the greatest admiration for single parents who have no one to support them day in, day out. For them there is no choice. But for a couple there are the benefits of supporting one another, of balancing each other off, and of being able to talk through the tough situations. Why not make the most of this benefit? If you are in a position where you are feeling undermined by the other, maybe the cause is an assumption that one of you is holding. Why not take the time to be introspective and see if there is something that simple at the root? Assumptions are deadly if they aren't brought out into the light.

POINTS TO PONDER

*1. Is there an assumption you or your spouse/
partner are not aware of that is affecting your
children?*

*2. Do you assume the children are someone else's
responsibility to correct?*

*3. Is there some issue from your childhood that
could be playing into your role as a parent?*

*4. Are you clear about the values you are hoping to
instil into your child?*

Stages

When I took my degree in education, one of the courses was focused on Piaget's Stages of Development. As a child matures physically they pass through different developmental phases. It is important to understand that they do, otherwise you will treat them as an adult. The problem is they do not think like an adult nor understand concepts and abstractions as an adult would. As a teen they are much more able to relate on this basis but as a two year old they aren't.

Words alone confuse children. Sarcasm is taken literally and words can simply be white noise to them. If your only strategy to train your children is reasoning with them, then you are wasting your time. Eventually they will understand your words but often by that time parents and children aren't even talking to each other.

If you are only using reasoning, you will keep repeating and repeating conversations that only prove that you are a nag. Nagging has never changed anyone. They may eventually conform for a time but although they are sitting on the outside they are standing on the inside. Nagging tends to reinforce wrong behaviour. I have met couples that have been experiencing marriage difficulties. One of them will accuse the other of constant nagging which they then confess only makes them more determined not to change. If adults take this stand, you can be sure your children will too. Nagging is usually a result of trying to impose a value that you hold upon someone else. If your training with your child is all word-based, they will not always understand what you are trying to tell them.

PARENTS: BEWARE!
RECOGNISE
CHILDREN GO
THROUGH DIFFERENT
DEVELOPMENT
STAGES

Training requires action. It requires that you demonstrate what you mean. If you want them to pick up their toys and put them in the toy box, then simply telling them to do it won't work. You need to demonstrate by showing them what your words mean. By doing it with them they learn what you mean. You may have to do this with them throughout their childhood. I remember as a teenager helping my father put an extension on our lakeside cottage. I was his "go-for". At one point he told me to get a 2x4. I took the measuring tape to the lumber stack and measured everyone in the pile looking for a 2x4. There wasn't one. So I returned empty handed at which point he royally told me off, as he was getting impatient waiting. He then went to the lumber pile and took the first board. I told him that was only 1 3/4 by 3 1/2. He explained to me that this was a 2x4 but the planer at the mill made the timber slightly smaller than 2x4. His rebuke smarted and was needless if he had only explained this first. His assumption was that I knew because I looked like a young man. I had another man tell me that he had the same experience with his dad when he was a teenager. It isn't a one-off type of experience.

Friends had a son who was extremely large for his age. At four he looked like an eight year old. He wasn't just tall but stocky too. His mother told us that he received a great deal of judgment from adults because they expected him to act much older than he actually was. It is the whole issue of assuming again. We assume that because they have a certain level of language mastery or physical size they can do or understand things they can't.

A child's perception isn't the same as an adult's. I remember as a child growing up in

Canada, the snow piled up to my waist. Now as an adult, I think it doesn't snow nearly as much because it is only up to my knees. The difference isn't necessarily global warming but more likely my change in height. As a 10 year old the garden that you asked them to rake looks like a football pitch. Tasks can feel overwhelming to them. Then they will whine and complain and not do the work. If all you do is rebuke the child with words, you will end up in a frustrating standoff. The thing to do is to recognise that the size of the project is intimidating them and that they need help. When we helped our children, they pitched in with enthusiasm because they knew nothing was impossible with the big people helping.

Children from birth to six years of age love routine. They are much better tempered if you don't mess with their routines. They get cranky if they change. They feel secure in the orderliness. Bonnie taught in a Montessori classroom for four and five year olds. They thrived on the routine. They learned many different skills but in a very ordered fashion. The routine included collecting the material required for an activity and was only considered complete when all the material was returned to its designated spot. The other thing about this age group is they need to have concrete stimuli to learn with. Counting and mathematical procedures are best learned using some form of material that can be manipulated. In North America the bread packages came with a plastic tag that sealed the bag. Those tags made terrific counters for such a lesson.

Whether Piaget would agree or not, we found the ages of six through ten to be the age of forgetfulness. At this age children cannot seem to retain more than one direction at a time. They either forget or become totally overwhelmed. In either case they never accomplish the second, third or subsequent thing on any list of directions. Tell them to do one thing at a time. When they are done, give them the next thing to do. When I returned to teaching after nine years of following other career paths, I told Bonnie that I had lost my skills as a teacher. I had a class of nine and ten year olds. One day I gave them a short assignment to do. Knowing that they would finish quickly, I also gave a list of work that they hadn't completed from the day before. I printed it on the blackboard so they could see what to do next. Some of the students sat there all day staring at the board with a glazed look on their faces. They actually did nothing. They weren't trouble in that they were misbehaving. They just simply didn't do a thing. Bonnie laughed when I told her what I had done. She suggested that I try giving them one thing at a time. She reminded me that I had spent the last nine years working with adults who had the capacity to handle such a list. When I used her strategy, everything worked fine. If we do the same thing with our own children, we could think they are being rebellious or lazy when in reality they are simply unable to handle this amount of information.

In situations that are created by not acknowledging certain limitations of age and development, we can end up in arguments with our children. It is futile to argue. They are the children and you are the parent. If you allow this to happen at an early age, it will only get worse with time. Don't be drawn into a battle of words. It will only aggravate you and lead to possible resentment for all involved. There is a time to answer the question why, and then there are times to simply say, "Do it because I told you to". At some point your child will keep asking "why?" just because they are stalling, not because they really don't understand. That is the point at which you need to say like a famous brand "Just Do It". But before you do, you also need to consider if it is any of the things that we have just shared. Are they overwhelmed? Do they not understand? Are they frustrated? Their response may well be from one of these problems and you would do well to rectify it rather than argue.

Arguing will make you feel under

pressure to cave in to their demands. Don't let it get to this point. Recognise what is happening and act in accordance with what is required. If you let your child go on and on, drawing you further and further into an argument, you will regret it. Words may be said that can't be retracted. A pattern may be developed that is eventually destructive to your relationship. To be drawn into an argument will bring nothing good. It is not a discussion. It is a battle in which the cause is all but lost. You need to be perceptive as to the source and deal with that. Do not let it escalate and become habitual. To allow arguing is to allow your child to dishonour you. Don't be drawn in.

Allowing arguing to be a part of your home life is neither healthy nor helpful. It creates an environment of stress and resentment. You wouldn't want a position of employment where the work environment is permeated with tension and constant arguing. Why allow this to be the situation in your home? As the parent you are the boss, the one who can do something about it. Arguing is not inevitable. It does not need to be accepted or tolerated.

Having raised four children to adulthood we know that you can have a home free of angry, argumentative children and teenagers. You may at times feel like you are trying to swim against the tide of popular opinion but what is popular is not always right. Dare to be different.

POINTS TO PONDER

1. Are you training through reasoning?

2. Do you find yourself repetitious and nagging?

*3. Have you overwhelmed your child or children
with too many tasks?*

*4. Do you argue with your child or children? If so,
how can you change this?*

The 26 Final Word

Parenting is a very demanding but very rewarding experience. It will not always be easy. The sleepless nights, the crying, the demands of a wilful child, or the shattered dreams of not having the perfect child are all part of the package. If someone had been able to tell you the truth, or if you had been able to receive the truth, would you have made a different choice? At the right moment, possibly! But when you look upon them asleep in their beds, your heart is still moved by how angelic they look and how deeply you love them.

A friend who had three children before we had any said to us that we would soon wonder how we could ever have been happy without them. At the time we couldn't comprehend that, but now I say "Amen". I look at the remainder of my life and think I am so happy to be facing it with a family that I love and who love me. The reward for running this race is lasting, enduring and eternal. What joy!

Material possessions and physical prowess all give way to time. What you had to have at thirty is a millstone around your neck at sixty. Your interests will change and your needs will change. But your family will remain forever. I attended a strategy meeting for an organisation that was looking to expand into Asia. During the discussion about what was the most appropriate action, what was the most necessary training and where was the most opportunity, a senior leader in his sixties made a statement that seemed out of context. He said, "At the end of the day after you have built all your plans you really only have your family and maybe a few, close friends." That hit me like a brick! I thought he had become cynical, disillusioned, tired or all of the above. It saddened me that at this point in his life, everything was reduced to only a small group of people.

I have pondered on this for a long time. I think he came to realise that only one thing really matters at the end of the day. It's your family. If you ignore it, you can gain everything materially but have nothing of truly lasting value. The saying 'blood is thicker than water' is so true. There is a filial bond that is stronger than any other. Family are the people who know you, love you and despite who you are, stick with you. They truly are worth the investment of time, energy and money.

Our desire for you is that you have a wonderful experience with your children. We desire that you and they can look back on their childhood with pleasure. That having a family isn't drudgery but a valuable fulfilling opportunity. Our hope and aim in writing this material was to provide you, the parent, with some practical hands-on skills. The very best thing you can do for yourself and for your children is to apply it. I have had the opportunity to teach people many different skills only to see them, after the initial glow wears off, ignore the new skills and plug on as before. What we have shared may require new thought patterns, new strategies, and radical changes. It will take some effort but persevere and the rewards will be great.

Remember: don't try to change everything all at once. The resulting chaos will guarantee failure and a return to the familiar. Change one thing at a time. Reward results lavishly with positive words of encouragement. Don't be in a rush. It took time to get to where you are. Be prepared to take the necessary time to establish new habits and patterns. It's like dieting. Everyone gains weight slowly but wants to lose it quickly. Flash in the pan results rarely last.

We brushed our children's teeth for five years and reminded them for seven more before they got it themselves. The reward for persevering was that none of them have had a cavity. So changing behaviour will some times take a little longer than we desire or we think. That's ok. Just don't quit.

Finally, take the time to enjoy the journey. It is lovely to have goals and plans but don't forsake the present for the future. They are only children for such a short time. Like a flower in bloom, enjoy the fragrance as much as possible before it is gone.

POINTS TO PONDER

1. What is the first behaviour you plan to change?

2. Do you have a strategy worked out?

3. Can you maintain consistency?

4. What positive words are you going to speak over your child to reinforce good behaviour and boost their confidence?

THE 24 SECRETS TO GREAT PARENTING

Change only one thing at a time...

1. What you value is where you put your time, energy and money.

2. Act on your words and do it consistently.

3. Know your child, for what works with one may not with the others.

4. Praise your children daily.

5. Be a keen observer of your child's behaviour.

6. Talk to your partner or a trusted friend for your sanity's sake!

7. Use a warning system and be prepared to respond if your child doesn't.

8. Take a break without your children for your sake and theirs.

9. Consistently act with a measured, calm response.

10. Forgiveness is essential and very powerful.

11. Start early to shape their personality.

12. Give your child the opportunity to choose from wisely determined choices.

13. Be aware that what your children watch will affect them.

14. Develop the ability to converse through asking your children open-ended questions.

15. Child rearing requires agreement by all the parents involved.

16. If correction is appropriate and applied consistently, it will create change.

17. Laugh and play with your children.

18. Words are powerful and can deeply affect your child.

19. The right choice for your child will not always make you popular.

20. You deserve what you tolerate.

21. Boundaries create security, protection and love.

22. Parenting is hard, labour intensive work that is best sustained by love.

23. Don't assume...discuss your individual expectations.

24. Parents: Beware! Recognise children go through different developmental stages.

...Enjoy the journey!

Jim & Bonnie HAPPY HOMES